*T*his volume is the first in a series of books dealing with American fighter pilots, and their aircraft, in the European Theatre of Operations during the Second World War. The exploits of Lightning, Thunderbolt and Mustang pilots flying 'starred-and-barred' fighters from 'Fortress Britain' will be detailed in the later titles in this series. The book you

ABOVE: Fighter pilots from No 71 'Eagle' Sqn stand proudly in front of one of their Hurricane Is at RAF Kirton-in-Lindsey on 17 March 1941.

presently hold in your hands focuses exclusively on those individuals who volunteered for action in war-torn Europe with the Royal Air Force prior to the American declaration of war, and the subsequent arrival of the US Army Air Forces in Britain.

Coverage of the early operations of VIII Fighter Command is also included up until its trio of Spitfire-equipped fighter groups either transitioned to the P-47 or were posted to the Mediterranean Theatre of Operations.

The large format of this book has allowed a substantial number of photographs of both men and their machinery to be included within its 128 pages. Sourced from both private and official archives, the photographs published in American Eagles represent the most comprehensive collection of early-war images of 'Yanks in Britain' ever published. Newly-commissioned profiles have also given an essentially 'black and white' war a colour dimension, and the majority of those aircraft depicted in artwork by leading British artist Mark Styling have been linked to notable pilots and/or events.

Although not attempting to be the definitive work on this little-publicised aspect of RAF Fighter Command (please check the comprehensive bibliography at the back of this volume for other works of note), American Eagles instead complements these textually-driven books through the sheer volume of photographs contained within its covers.

The mix of images, first-hand accounts and thoroughly researched text and captions should make this volume a useful reference tool for historians, aviation enthusiasts and hobbyists alike.

Tony Holmes, January 2001

Pre-War Pilots

At the end of the First World War, the recently-created Royal Air Force possessed the largest fleet of aircraft of any of the combatant nations involved in the conflict. It comprised approximately 3500 aircraft and no fewer than 290,000 men and women, split between 188 frontline and 187 training units. Despite having helped win the war, the world's first independent air service had been stripped of almost 90 per cent of its personnel within 15 months of the armistice.

By March 1920, an emasculated RAF could boast just 25 operational squadrons, of which only seven were actually based in the UK. That same year the 'peace-time' air force was allotted an annual 'rebuilding' budget of just £15-million for the next five years. In comparison, its daily expenditure during the final year of the war had been £1-million, and £54-million had been spent on demobilising and disbanding the RAF in 1919-20!

The paltry defence budget reflected the Coalition government's feeling that Britain and her empire would be unlikely to fight another major war for at least a decade. Dubbed the 'Ten Years' Rule', this assumption allowed the Treasury to deny the spending of money on preparations for potential future conflicts. Such a policy remained in effect until 1932.

The folly of this rule was revealed as early as 1923, when the newly-elected Conservative government realised that there was a rapidly growing disparity between British and French air strengths. At that time France was considered to be the only country in Europe capable of maintaining strong military and naval forces, and therefore pose a threat to the sovereignty of the UK. The Cabinet reacted by immediately embarking upon a new scheme of expansion that would see the establishment of a metropolitan air force of 52 squadrons. However, senior RAF officers informed the government that such a strength could not be attained for at least five years. Of these 52 squadrons, 13 of them would be non-regular units of the Auxiliary Air Force and Special Reserve.

By mid-1932 just 42 units had been established, and with the election of Adolf Hitler as German chancellor barely six months later, followed by his bold policy of rapid militarisation, the parlous state of the RAF's re-equipment programme was soon brought into sharp focus.

Indeed, the newly-formed *Luftwaffe* could boast at least 22 frontline units of fighters and bombers by the end of 1934, which controlled approximately 560 aircraft. These figures effectively matched the RAF's frontline force in Britain at the time, although the Germans had

BELOW RIGHT: Flying in a textbook Aircraft Close Vic formation (although with too great a distance between the flights for them to be considered to be in Sections Close Vic), six immaculate Aluminium-doped Hawker Harts of No 601 'County of London' Sqn cruise serenely over Middlesex in the autumn of 1936. Each aircraft bears the unit's distinctive 'flying sword' emblem on its fin, which was applied in letterbox red. The 'fighter bars' on either side of the fuselage roundel and on the upper wing surface also employed letterbox red, although this time in the shape of triangles, mirrored in black. Finally, the wheel covers on each aircraft are painted royal blue to denote their assignment to 'B' Flight's 'Blue' Section – 'Green', 'Yellow' and 'Red' Sections all flew Harts marked accordingly. All three of the aircraft in the formation closest to the camera had been delivered to No 601 Sqn directly from Hawker and Armstrong-Whitworth in 1933.

ABOVE: These Gauntlet IIs of No 79 Sqn were photographed at RAF Northolt, in Middlesex, during a visit to the station in the early spring of 1938. The airfield was popular with fighter units from No 11 Group at this time, for resident No 111 Sqn was then in the process of converting onto the first Hawker Hurricanes to enter frontline service. Biplane pilots were naturally keen to see their future monoplane mounts 'in the flesh'.

already embarked on an expansion plan to double this strength as quickly as possible. No such comparable programme existed for the RAF. The lack of any such plan infuriated future Prime Minister Winston Churchill, whose attacks on the government eventually resulted in the adoption of 'Scheme C' in 1935.

The bare bones of this plan stipulated that funds would be made available for a UK-based force of 79 bomber and 35 fighter squadrons, all of which were to be operational by 1942. The bomber 'bias' reflected the contemporary view that future aerial warfare would see the bomber units of opposing nations battling it out in a war of attrition, with fighters being left to protect their bases from attack.

Due to the planned increase in the frontline strength of the RAF, the service was divided into four new commands as part of 'Scheme C' so as to allow it to be administered more effectively. Bomber, Coastal, Fighter and Training Commands were thus created.

Fighter Command assumed the duties of its immediate predecessor, Air Defence of Great Britain (ADGB), on 14 July 1936, and at its helm was placed Air Marshal H C T Dowding. A veteran of combat in the First World War and in Palestine during the 1920s, Dowding was the ideal man for the job due to his previous command of RAF Inland Area, which was the fighter group within the now-defunct ADGB. In the six years prior to becoming Air Officer Commanding Fighter Command, Dowding had served as Air Member for Supply and Research to the Air Council.

In this role, he had overseen the implementation of numerous tenders to private industry that directly resulted in the RAF's eventual procurement of both the Hawker Hurricane and the Supermarine Spitfire, as well as personally encouraging the development of radio direction finding (RDF), which later became known as radar. These three elements would all prove crucial come the summer of 1940.

"The Millionaires' Club"

The fighter pilots serving in the RAF at the time of the creation of Fighter Command in mid-1936 were very much the 'glamour boys' of the air force. The subject of adulation in the press, and the envy of thousands of schoolboys across the country, those young men who succeeded in gaining their 'wings' and joining a biplane fighter unit were at the pinnacle of their profession. Amongst that select band who flew fighters within the pre-war RAF were four Americans – James

ABOVE:
Devoid of any distinguishing unit markings, Gauntlet II K7885 is seen at RAF North Coates, on the Lincolnshire coast south of Grimsby, during No 79 Sqn's annual Armament Practice Camp in the late summer of 1937. Amongst the first batch of Gauntlet IIs delivered to the unit upon its formation in March of that year, this aircraft was subsequently passed on to No 601 Sqn in December of 1938 following No 79 Sqn's conversion onto the Hurricane. In turn replaced within the auxiliary squadron by a Blenheim I in late March 1939, the fighter then spent time in a succession of maintenance units, before being sent to the air depot at RAF Aboukir, in Egypt, four months later. Assigned to No 102 Maintenance Unit (MU), K7885 was lost within days of arriving in the Middle East when an aileron rod failed whilst it was in flight on 17 July 1939. The aircraft dived into the ground near Abu Sueir, west of the Suez Canal, killing the pilot.

William Elias Davies, Carl Raymond Davis, Cyril Dampier 'Pussy' Palmer and Willard Whitney Straight.

Aside from Straight, who became a British citizen in 1936, it is almost certain that the remaining trio each held dual US/British citizenship, for Palmer and Davies had British parents, and all four individuals had been schooled in the UK prior to joining the air force. Of this quartet, the first to don the blue-grey uniform of the RAF was 25-year-old Carl Davis, who joined the Royal Auxiliary Air Force in 1936.

Born in South Africa to American parents, Davis enjoyed the benefits of a public school education from the age of 13, attending Sherborne School and Trinity College, in Cambridge. Upon graduation, Davis returned to the USA and enrolled in McGill University, where he qualified as a mining engineer. Having completed his degree, he duly returned to the UK.

Being a young man of some financial means, and a keen private pilot, Davis joined the auxiliary air force once back in England – his 'local' squadron was No 601 'County of London' Sqn, based at RAF Hendon. One of the first five units established with the formation of the Royal Auxiliary Air Force in 1925, No 601 Sqn had been staffed from the start by 'well to do' gentlemen from the capital and the surrounding home counties. Such was the reputation created by the unit that it soon became known in the RAF as 'The Millionaires' Mob'!

By the time Carl Davis was commissioned as a pilot officer in the auxiliary air force on 7 August 1936, No 601 Sqn had been equipped with the sleek Hawker Hart light bomber for more than three years. Painted silver overall, and distinctively marked with green and black 'fighter bands' on the fuselage and upper wing, the Harts had become a familiar sight in the skies of south-east England, as the squadron exercised at various fighter bases within No 11 Group. Within 12 months of Davis's arrival at Hendon, his unit had replaced its Harts with the closely related Demon, which boasted a Frazer-Nash hydraulic turret for the gunner sat behind the pilot.

The brotherly fraternity that characterised No 601 Sqn pre-war was further reinforced by

BELOW: Undoubtedly the finest looking RAF fighter of its generation, the Hawker Fury gave the air force great service throughout the 1930s. Six fighter squadrons were equipped with the aircraft, No 43 Sqn receiving its first examples in May 1931 and No 41 Sqn discarding its last Furies in January 1939. This quartet belong to No 1 Sqn, which transitioned from Armstrong-Whitworth Siskins to Furies at RAF Tangmere in February 1932. All four fighters boast the letterbox red fighter bars synonymous with the 'Fighting First', as well as the 'winged one' emblem on their respective fins. K5673 also has a solid red fin and tailplane, denoting its assignment to the commander of 'A' Flight. This photograph was taken by the legendary Charles E Brown sometime after No 1 Sqn had revised its squadron badge in the summer of 1936.

"... a pretty wild and high-spirited gathering"

MAX AITKEN

Life in the pre-war auxiliaries was viewed by most officers as akin to belonging to a uniformed flying club. Although the views and experiences of Carl Davis were never committed to print, one of his squadronmates, The Honourable John William Maxwell Aitken (who became an ace during the Second World War, and was subsequently knighted in 1965), succinctly described 'The Millionaires' Mob' in the following quote, published in his official papers in 1982:

'One day in 1934 a friend of mine, Roger Bushell, said to me *"Why don't you join the Auxiliary Air Force, Max?"* Bushell was one of a group of excellent skiers of my acquaintance, an adventurous, hell-raising collection of men who, at the right time of year, would cross the Channel with their cars and drive fast down the highway to St Anton, where I had a house. Bushell also flew. The idea of flying an aircraft attracted me very much, and when Bushell said: *"I'll arrange for you to meet Philip Sassoon at lunch"*, I at once agreed. Sir Philip Sassoon at the time was Under-Secretary of State for Air, with a special interest in the Auxiliary air squadrons. I met him, liked him very much and, in consequence, I found myself posted to No 601 Fighter Squadron, with its headquarters at Hendon.

'My companions there were, as you would expect, a pretty wild and high-spirited gathering, many of whom I already knew from skiing – and after-skiing – parties at St Anton. They were the sort of young men who had not quite been expelled from their schools, whom mothers warned their daughters against – in vain – who stayed up far too late at parties and then, when everyone was half dead with fatigue, went on to other parties. Does that sort of young man still exist? I do not know. But in those days they were quite common. And they clustered in unusual density at the headquarters of No 601 Sqn.'

LEFT: The Honourable Max Aitken is seen here as a flying officer at Tangmere just prior to the *Blitzkrieg* in France in May 1940. A member of No 601 Sqn from September 1935, Canadian-born Aitken was CO of the unit by the time he was posted out of the frontline on 20 July 1940, having being credited with seven victories and awarded the Distinguished Flying Cross (DFC). During subsequent frontline postings he enjoyed further aerial successes flying Spitfires and Beaufighters, finishing the war as a group captain with 14 and 1 shared victories, and a Distinguished Service Order (DSO).

marriage, for in 1938 Carl Davis was betrothed to the sister of squadronmate Sir Archibald Hope, and Hope in turn to Davis's sister. Several other pilots also took wives who were the sisters or cousins of fellow members of the 'Millionaires' Mob', which caused confirmed bachelor Roger Bushell to remark: '*If this sort of thing goes on much longer, this squadron will be as in-bred as an Austrian village*'.

By then Carl Davis was not the only American serving with No 601 Sqn, for in 1937 famous US-born millionaire racing car driver, aircraft designer and accomplished private pilot Willard Whitney Straight had joined the unit after becoming a British citizen the previous year. The nephew of Lord Queenborough, and a graduate of Cambridge, Straight had spent many years studying art in Munich, where he had seen at first-hand the rise of German militarism. Convinced that Nazism had to be stopped at all costs, he had joined the auxiliaries and awaited the call to arms.

By December of 1938, No 601 Sqn had begun to replace its thoroughly obsolete Demons with marginally less antiquated Gloster Gauntlet II biplane fighters. These aircraft arrived on the squadron already camouflaged in dark green and dark earth, having served previously with either Nos 32 or 79 Sqns at Biggin Hill. Hastily repainted during the Munich Crisis of the previous September, the Gauntlets appeared far more war-like than the aluminium-

BELOW LEFT: Altering formation from a tight 'tucked in' diamond to a close echelon to starboard, the quartet of No 1 Sqn Furies are captured on film once again by Charles E Brown. The aircraft furthest from the camera is something of a mystery machine, for it clearly wears the serial K2040 aft of the fuselage roundel in the diamond formation photo, yet in this shot it is marked with the serial K2039! In an effort to further obscure its true identity, the fighter lacks any serial whatsoever on its rudder. After consulting Air Ministry movement cards, the Author believes that this Fury I is in fact K2039, for K2040 was reportedly issued to No 6 Flying Training School (FTS) at RAF Netheravon, in Wiltshire, on the last day of October 1935.

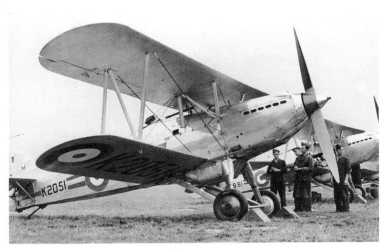

ABOVE: K2051 and K2881 sit chocked on the flightline at Tangmere during the summer of 1937. Although both fighters had spent almost five years in the frontline by the time this photograph was taken, neither exhibit any signs of weariness. K2051 had been issued to No 1 Sqn straight from Hawker's Kingston factory on 20 February 1932, and remained with the unit until 29 April 1936. Following two months in storage, it was then returned to Tangmere and issued to No 43 Sqn on 1 July, although exactly four weeks later K2051 was transferred to No 25 Sqn at RAF Hawkinge. The latter unit transitioned to Fury IIs in November of that year, and the Fury I was duly sent back to No 1 Sqn. Here it remained until redesignated an instructional maintenance airframe (1017M) on 30 November 1937. K2881 served exclusively with No 1 Sqn from 3 February 1934 until irreparably damaged in a landing accident with K8275 at Tangmere on 23 February 1938.

finished and 'fighter bar'-bedecked Demons, which were now passed on to Training Command.

Meanwhile, No 601 Sqn had been mobilised (on 26 September 1938) during the Munich Crisis and sent to Biggin Hill, where it remained until ordered back to Hendon on 31 October.

The unit's initial flirtation with single-seat fighters was to last just a matter of weeks, for in January 1939 the first Bristol Blenheim IF 'heavy' fighters arrived at Hendon. Unlike the weary ex-Fighter Command Gauntlets they replaced, the twin-engined Blenheims were fresh off the Bristol production line at Filton, and the squadron wasted no time in adorning them with its distinctive 'UF' codes and winged sword emblem.

The culmination of the squadron's transition onto the Blenheim came in August 1939 at the unit's annual 14-day summer training camp, which on this occasion was held at Ford, near Tangmere, on the Sussex coast. Previously viewed as little more than a summer 'outing' by members of No 601 Sqn, this year's camp was viewed far more seriously, for war against Germany now seemed almost certain. Indeed, within days of returning to Hendon the unit was mobilised, its Blenheims being sent to Biggin Hill on 2 September. The 'Millionaires' Mob', including Flg Offs Carl Davis and Whitney Straight, now prepared themselves for war.

BELOW: Originally flown by Officer Commanding No 1 Sqn, Sqn Ldr Charles Spackman, following its delivery to the unit on 10 February 1932, K2048 was later passed on to one of the flight commanders (exactly which one remains unclear). When flown by the boss, the fighter's No 1 Sqn spearhead was replaced by the CO's traditional rectangular rank pennant painted onto an all-Aluminium fin. K2048 went on to serve with No 25 Sqn, and it was eventually grounded on 10 December 1937.

Fighter Command

With the arrival of No 601 Sqn at Biggin Hill, the resident population of American pilots trebled, for serving with No 79 Sqn was James Davies. Born in Bernardsville, New Jersey, Davies had returned to the UK with his parents sometime prior to him joining the RAF in early 1936. Upon gaining his 'wings', he was posted to the newly-reformed No 79 Sqn at Biggin Hill in March 1937.

This unit had been created as part of 'Scheme C', its nucleus of pilots and groundcrew coming from long-term Biggin Hill residents, No 32 Sqn. The latter unit simply transferred its entire 'B Flight' to the new squadron, whilst the remaining complement of pilots arrived fresh from flying training schools and a handful of other units. Its Gauntlet II biplane fighters were sourced from a variety of frontline units, including Nos 17, 32, 54, 56 and 111 Sqns, although

LEFT: K8249 was one of thirteen Fury IIs supplied to No 1 Sqn in early 1937, the improved version of Hawker's classic biplane fighter boasting a top speed of 223 mph, as opposed to the Mk I's 207 mph. One of five Mk IIs transferred to the unit from No 73 Sqn following the latter outfit's transition onto the Gladiator, K8249 remained with No 1 Sqn until the arrival of Hurricane's at Tangmere in October 1938. Passed on to No 26 MU, the Fury II became instructional airframe 1547M on 7 June 1939.

ABOVE: No 1 Sqn was in the process of converting onto the Hurricane I when 'Flight' paid a visit to Tangmere, so it could not participate in the aerial photography session. However, its Fury IIs were identically camouflaged, although they lacked the traditional fighter spearhead worn by the aircraft of No 43 Sqn. Seen in Aircraft Close Vic, Sections Close Vic formation, the aircraft all lack serials, bar 'Red 2' in the leader's section. On the original print, the serial K8297 can be made out on the all-white starboard underwing section.

the bulk of its airframes – 11 in total – were newly-built aircraft that had been delivered straight from the Gloster factory at Hucclecote to No 1 Aircraft Storage Unit (ASU) at Waddington. These ex-No 1 ASU Gauntlets were amongst the very last examples built for the RAF.

Painted in the standard overall 'Aluminium (silver) dope on all fabric-covered areas, without polished metal areas', as per King's regulations, No 79 Sqn adopted a distinctive red arrow as its unit marking, the shaft of which passed 'through' the fuselage roundel. Like No 32 Sqn, the new unit immediately set about the daily routine that was the lot of Fighter Command squadrons in the final 18 months prior to the Munich Crisis.

Early every morning groundcrews would wheel the serviceable Gauntlets out of the No 79 Sqn hangar and line the fighters up on the tarmac, wing-tip to wing-tip. Sometime after 09.00

LEFT:
In the wake of heightened tension between Britain and Germany over the latter country's occupation of the Sudetenland in August 1938, Fighter Command frantically ordered that all its frontline types should be camouflaged forthwith. A contingency plan for the repainting of combat aircraft in war emergency paint schemes had been formulated in 1936 by the Air Staff, and this was now brought into effect. All upper surfaces were painted Dark Green and Dark Earth in either Scheme A or the mirror-imaged Scheme B, whilst the under surfaces were finished in the Night (black) and White scheme. All Furies at Tangmere were repainted accordingly, and in October 1938 No 43 Sqn sortied 12 of its Mk IIs for the benefit of a visiting 'Flight' photographer.

the unit would take-off, after which it would perform air attack practice, air firing, cross-country navigation, formation flying or mock interceptions of other service aircraft in the vicinity of Biggin Hill. Occasionally pilots would fly twice in the morning and once in the afternoon, although as a general rule the latter period was usually set aside for maintenance of aircraft.

A great rivalry soon built up between the two fighter units at Biggin Hill, for both squadrons flew Gauntlets, and a goodly number of pilots in No 79 Sqn had previously served with No 32 Sqn. Members of the 'senior' unit protested that they had 'fathered a shocking miscarriage', and the competition between the two squadrons came to a head in the blazing sun of the Empire Air Day in 1937. This is how Graham Wallace described the event in his volume *RAF Biggin Hill*, published in 1957:

'Nearly 20,000 people visited the station. Nos 32 and 79 Sqns competed against each other in a medley of events, honours being equally divided, the most spectacular being the reach for altitude. In the wonderful clear weather the Gauntlets could be seen with the naked eye at 20,000 ft.'

Despite being the star turn at the air day, the ineffectiveness of the biplane fighter as a modern weapon of war had been graphically revealed during the annual air exercises held by Fighter Command that very same summer. The 'invading' force had included some newly-delivered Blenheim I bombers in its ranks, and the Gauntlet pilots at Biggin Hill had

ABOVE: Merlin engines throbbing and groundcrew standing to attention, a trio of Hurricane Is from No 79 Sqn's 'B' Flight idle on the ramp in front of the North Camp triple-bay Belfast hangar at Biggin Hill in 1939. These early-production examples of Hawker's monoplane fighter were fitted with two-bladed, fixed-pitch wooden airscrews, fabric-covered wings and no windscreen or seat armour. The aircraft closest to the camera is L1718/'AL-T', which was amongst the batch of 17 Hurricane Is delivered new to No 79 Sqn from Hawker's Brooklands facility in November 1938. Passed on to No 111 Sqn in late 1939, this aircraft was reportedly lost in France during the Blitzkrieg of May 1940, although the exact details of its final demise remain unrecorded.

suffered the humiliation of watching the Bristol monoplanes effortlessly pull away from the struggling biplane fighters when they had attempted to effect an interception.

Although both units were designated as day fighter squadrons, night flying also began to feature more prominently in pilots' logbooks come 1938. Such sorties were encouraged by no less an individual that Air Marshal Dowding himself, who proclaimed on his numerous visits to Biggin Hill, '*I'm only interested in nightflying and dirty weather*'.

On 12 April 1938, No 79 Sqn exhibited its nocturnal prowess when it performed Fighter Command's first night formation flight. Nine Gauntlets took off singly into the inky blackness and joined up at 6,000 ft over Sevenoaks in squadron formation. Flying wing-tip to wing-tip, eyes glued to red station keeping-lights, the pilots then headed due north to the Thames and followed the river down to Sheerness, before completing an arc over Hornchurch, Uxbridge, Epsom, Kenley and finally back to Biggin Hill. Flg Off Davies participated in this historic sortie, and was also a part of a follow-up formation flight made later that month.

On 5 August 1938 the peacetime routine of Biggin Hill's fighter squadrons came to a sudden halt with the flashing of the code-word '*Diabolo*' from Fighter Command HQ at Bentley Priory to the station commander, Wg Cdr H G W 'Fiery' Lock. This instructed him to bring Biggin Hill to a state of 'immediate readiness for war'. This signal was sent in response to Germany's imminent invasion of the demilitarised Sudetenland. The Munich Crisis had started.

No 79 Sqn was absent at the time, with its pilots and groundcrew enjoying a week's leave. However, all personnel were soon recalled, and one of their first jobs was to camouflage the Gauntlets. Along with the disappearance of the red arrow went the squadron crest – a 'Salamander salient in flames' – emblazoned on the fin of each fighter.

In the midst of the crisis, a Miles Magister monoplane trainer flew in to the station on 11 August in preparation for the arrival of the first Hurricanes assigned to Biggin Hill. Five weeks later No 32 Sqn took delivery of its first Hawker fighters, and No 79 Sqn would re-equip in November. Although pilots initially viewed the appreciably larger, and less manoeuvrable, Hurricane with suspicion, after a flight or two in the monoplane fighter, few lamented the passing of the Gauntlet.

Personnel from both units now worked hard to become fully conversant with the capabilities of their new mount, familiarising themselves with increased closing speeds for interceptions,

BELOW LEFT: With the expansion of Fighter Command in the last years of peace, the major fighter stations across the UK started making use of satellite fields, which would operate as the temporary home for frontline units. The idea behind this was to allow Fighter Command to disperse its forces in advance of major bases coming under sustained attack. Taking Biggin Hill as an example, should it have been rendered unusable, its units could have continued to defend the region from a series of austere sites that had previously operated as private aerodromes. These two No 79 Sqn Hurricane Is are seen at just such a location in mid-1939 – Gravesend Airport. Strategically placed on high ground overlooking the Thames, Gravesend would become one of No 11 Group's key airfields. Indeed, the first RAF presence at the site was established as early as 1937, when No 20 Elementary and Reserve Flying Training school was formed to train both air force and Fleet Air Arm pilots.

engagements at higher altitudes, a variable two-speed propeller, retractable undercarriage and radio transmitters that worked over far greater distances. The tactics employed by Fighter Command were still much the same as they had been in the biplane fighter era, however, and a seemingly endless series of interception flights was performed under the guidance of Biggin Hill's fighter controllers.

By the end of the annual summer exercises in August 1939, the pilots of Nos 32 and 79 Sqns considered themselves ready for war. Just twelve months earlier they had been at the controls of biplanes little removed from the Sopwith Camels and Snipes which their famous forebears had flown into combat over the Western Front in 1918. Now a new generation of pilots prepared to do battle in monoplane fighters that were the equal of any designs then in frontline service.

'Foremost in Everything'

ABOVE: 'No 79 Squadron, Scramble!' Although staged for the attendant press corps at Biggin Hill on Tuesday, 8 August 1939, this shot nevertheless captures the mood of the final peacetime Air Defence Exercises. Exactly twelve months later fighter pilots would be repeating the self-same routine several times a day, although they were now intercepting real Luftwaffe aircraft in their hundreds, rather than a handful of Blenheim Is hastily repainted with white crosses.

The last of the quartet of American pilots to reach the frontline was Cyril Dampier 'Pussy' Palmer, who was born in Cleveland, Ohio, in March 1918. Barely 20 when he received his 'wings', Palmer was posted to No 1 Sqn at RAF Tangmere during the summer of 1938.

The oldest unit in the air force, and revelling in the motto *'In omnibus princeps'* ('Foremost in everything'), No 1 Sqn had built up an envious reputation for precision flying with its now thoroughly antiquated Hawker Fury Is. Perhaps the most famous of all interwar RAF fighters, the Furies had been on strength with the unit for over six years, and No 1 Sqn had called Tangmere home since February 1927.

Many of the unit's more experienced pilots had been posted away during the first six months of 1938 following the completion of their respective tours, and they had, in turn, been replaced by newly 'winged' individuals like 'Pussy' Palmer. These tyro fighter pilots had little time to get to get to grips with life in a frontline unit, however, for war with Germany seemed inevitable with every passing month.

The training regime on which Plt Off Palmer embarked during the summer of 1938 was detailed by ex-squadron pilot Michael Shaw in his 1971 volume *No 1 Squadron*:

'New pilots arriving on the Squadron were subjected to an intensive course in air combat. Whatever their background, they were left in little doubt of their lowly place in the scheme of things. It took several months for a new boy to win an accepted place in the bosom of the unit, and it was soon obvious to all if one of them was not making the grade. The new pilots now arriving were a very cosmopolitan crew. Some, like Sgt Bill Berry from No 43, were seasoned regulars, but they were being joined in increasing numbers by volunteers from the wider world. Plt Off Billy Drake from London, Leslie Clisby from Adelaide and 'Pussy' Palmer from Cleveland, Ohio, were among the new faces of 1938.

'It was up to those at the top end of the Squadron to knock off their rough edges and mould them into the collective image without dampening their enthusiasm or killing their spirit.'

Within weeks of Palmer's arrival the Sudetenland crisis erupted, and life at Tangmere drastically changed for the resident fighter units, Nos 1 and 43 Sqns. Everything was camouflaged, including both aircraft and hangars, air raid shelters were dug, all leave was cancelled and flying took place at the station all day long following the abandonment of the 'tropical routine'. Tangmere was the only station in

BELOW: Once in the air, No 79 Sqn formed up into Aircraft Close Line Abreast formation, and proceeded to fly over the North Downs at medium altitude for the benefit of the press photographers aloft in an RAF Anson. This particular shot, again taken on 8 August 1939, was captured by the 'Kent Messenger' photographer. The aircraft closest to the camera, L1697/'AL-A', was the personal mount of No 79 Sqn's CO, Sqn Ldr C C McMullen, who led the unit from January 1939 through to February 1940. The Hurricane fifth from bottom is L1716/'AL-D', which was regularly flown by Flg Off James Davies.

Hawker Hurricane I L1716 of No 79 Sqn, Biggin Hill, August 1939
This aircraft was flown by Flg Off J W E Davies during the final peacetime RAF Air Defence
Exercises, held in August 1939. Delivered new to No 79 Sqn in December 1938, it remained in
RAF service until struck off charge in July 1944.

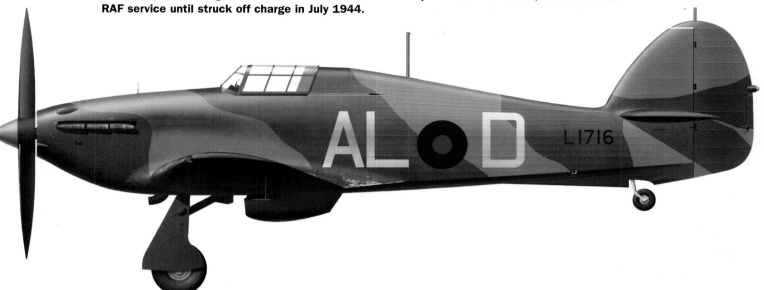

the UK to observe this routine, which was practised by the RAF abroad during the summer
months at its various bases across the Empire. Squadrons would launch their first flights of the
day shortly after 07.30 hrs, and then fly intensely until 13.00 hrs, when the station stood down
for the day.

The Sudetenland crisis also revealed fundamental inadequacies with the Fury that a lick of
paint and round-the-clock flying could not conceal. To start with, both squadrons were suffering
from a chronic shortage of belted ammunition for the fighter's twin Vickers 0.303-in machine
guns – it was discovered that each fighter had just two belts per gun! And with no belt-
positioning machines available, officers and men alike worked in shifts hand-tapping single
rounds into belts with large spanners. Sadly, the Fury's lack of performance could not be
rectified so simply.

Once the fastest fighter in the RAF with a top speed of 220 mph, the Hawker biplane was
now the slowest. No 1 Sqn's CO, Sqn Ldr Ian Bertram, instructed his pilots to attack incoming
enemy aircraft head-on, and finished his briefing with the following order: *'Gentlemen, our
aircraft are too slow to catch the German bombers: we must ram them'*.

Fortunately for the men of Nos 1 and 43 Sqns, and the rest of the nation, Prime Minister
Neville Chamberlain returned from a meeting in Munich with Adolf Hitler in late September
having staved off outright war with Germany for another twelve precious months.

No 1 Sqn continued with its intensive flying programme into the late autumn of 1938, Sqn
Ldr Bertram being anxious to derive as much training value as possible from his Furies prior to
the arrival of Hurricane Is. These sorties took the form of mock dogfights with No 43 Sqn, or
practice interceptions of No 217 Sqn Ansons, which patrolled the south coast from Tangmere.

On 15 October the squadron was instructed to send three pilots to Hawker's Brooklands
factory to familiarise themselves with the new
fighter. After being talked through the controls,
the trio flew the Hurricanes back to Tangmere.
Further aircraft were collected in twos and
threes from the manufacturer over the coming
weeks, and by 7 November No 1 Sqn had its
full complement of Hurricane Is.

By March 1939 all squadron pilots were
rated operational with the new fighter, which
they found handled just as well as the Fury.
The Hurricane had a top speed of around 320
mph, however, and was armed with eight
rather than two 0.303-in machine guns. Such

BELOW: Yet another
participant in the
August 1939 exercises
was Hurricane I
L1719/'AL-F', which is
seen here at Gravesend
undergoing minor
maintenance on its
port undercarriage leg.
This aircraft was
written off in a belly-
landing on 13 April
1940 at Biggin Hill after
its engine cut out on
take-off.

RIGHT: No 1 Sqn became 'Brighton's Own' in 1939 as part of an Air Ministry scheme instigated to link RAF units with nearby towns and cities. The first opportunity that citizens of the Sussex city had to visit their 'own' fighter squadron came in June of that year during the annual Empire Air Day. Tens of thousands flocked to the station, and the highlight of the event was the 15-aircraft close formation flypast performed by No 1 Sqn, the unit being led through a series of low diving manoeuvres by its CO, Sqn Ldr P J H 'Bull' Halahan. These No 1 Sqn Hurricanes were photographed just prior to taking off for the formation flypast on Empire Air Day.

LEFT: Hooked up to an Albion AM463 triple-hose bowser, a Hurricane I of No 1 Sqn is refuelled on the line at Tangmere in early 1939. Note how the engine cowling fasteners have already become chipped and the paintwork aft of the exhaust stubs blackened within weeks of the Hurricane's arrival in the frontline from the Hawker factory. These telltale signs of heavy use indicate just how hard No 1 Sqn pushed itself to achieve operational readiness with the new fighter during the winter of 1938-39.

performance captured the imagination of the press, as Michael Shaw related in the following quote from *No 1 Squadron*:

'One newspaper ran a story about the new breed of supermen who were being specially developed by the RAF to fly its new fighters. These pilots, it was claimed, were abstemious of all vices. Their biceps bulged and their hands were gnarled with wrestling with the controls of their Hurricanes. This news was received at Tangmere with the hoots of mirth it deserved. Abstemious indeed! The publicans and fathers of Sussex had good cause to know otherwise.'

During the final months of peace, No 1 Sqn continued to hone its skills with the Hurricane, attending an air firing practice camp at RAF Sutton Bridge, in Lincolnshire, in late May. Night flying also regularly appeared on the operational schedule following the introduction of searchlight batteries in southern England, as did pioneering day-time interceptions through the use of RDF (radar) stations scattered along the south coast. In August the last peacetime Air Exercises took place, and No 1 Sqn was heavily committed to the numerous sorties flown against 'enemy' bombers attempting to penetrate No 11 Group's airspace.

Soon after the completion of the exercise, all fighter pilots at Tangmere were briefed on the strength of the *Luftwaffe* by the British Assistant Air Attaché in Berlin, Sqn Ldr Coop, and what he told them left them stunned. German airpower far exceeded the RAF's current frontline strength, and unbeknown to the pilots of No 1 Sqn, war was just a matter of days away.

RIGHT: Another photograph from the sequence taken on the Empire Air Day in June 1939. With No 1 Sqn succeeding in putting all 15 of its aircraft into the air on this occasion, it is almost certain that Plt Off 'Pussy' Palmer participated in the memorable event. Note how none of the Hurricanes seen in these Empire Air Day photos seem to be marked with serials.

LEFT: Plt Off 'Pussy' Palmer (centre) is seen in a casual pose with other No 1 Sqn pilots outside the unit's Watch Office at Tangmere during the summer of 1939. Behind the American are Flg Offs S W Baldie and C G H 'Leak' Crusoe, whilst the individual scratching his head is Flt Lt P R 'Johnny' Walker, the squadron's senior flight commander. A member of No 1 Sqn's legendary 1937 Hendon Air Pageant aerobatic team, Walker enjoyed great success during the Phoney War and the Battle of France, claiming a number of victories (including a half-share in the destruction of the first Bf 110 downed by an RAF fighter). Awarded a DFC in June 1940, followed by the DSO in August 1942, Walker survived the conflict with a final tally of three and two shared destroyed, two unconfirmed destroyed and one damaged.

RIGHT: This worm's eye shot of Hurricane I 'NA-G' was taken at HMS *Peregine*, better known as Royal Naval Air Station Ford, in mid-1939. Situated just a few miles west of Tangmere on the Sussex coast, this airfield was a regular destination for No 1 Sqn Hurricanes on navigation exercises during the final months of peace. 'NA-G's' serial remains a mystery, although it is known that the fighter was frequentlly flown by Plt Off 'Pussy' Palmer during this time.

Hawker Hurricane I (serial unknown) of No 1 Sqn, Tangmere, June 1939
Painted in a typical RAF pre-war fighter camouflage scheme, this Hurricane I was
regularly flown by Plt Off C D 'Pussy' Palmer during the final months of peace in Europe.

'Phoney War', *Blitzkrieg* and *Dynamo*

In the early hours of 1 September 1939 the German army invaded Poland, supported by the massed ranks of the *Luftwaffe*. The governments of Britain and France challenged this act of aggression, having verbally promised the Polish people the previous March that they would not be abandoned to their fate. Prime Minister Neville Chamberlain immediately gave the Germans an ultimatum, stating that if the invading troops were not removed by 11.00 hrs on Sunday, 3 September, a state of war would exist between the two countries. The *Führer* refused to remove his forces, and the British government duly declared war on Germany. France followed suit six hours later.

Arrangements had been made in the summer by the British and French governments for the rapid deployment of the British Expeditionary Force (BEF) following the outbreak of war. Fighter cover for the troops that would head across the Channel was to be initially provided by four squadrons of Hurricanes, one of which was No 1 Sqn.

Air Chief Marshal Hugh Dowding was vehemently opposed to the removal of these units from Fighter Command, and on the day Germany invaded Poland, he visited Tangmere to see how No 1 Sqn's preparations for war were progressing. As he viewed the unit's rush to get its equipment ready for a possible move, he turned to the squadron's commanding officer, Sqn Ldr 'Bull' Halahan, and remarked, 'I am very sorry indeed to lose No 1 Sqn. If war breaks out and you go to France, you may take only 12 aircraft and the pilots you have. You can expect no reinforcement from me.'

BELOW RIGHT:
This Hurricane I of No 1 Sqn was almost certainly photographed at Tangmere around the time of the German invasion of Poland. Note the fighter's Type A1 fuselage roundel, which was applied at the factory on new Hurricanes, then abandoned during the Munich Crisis of September 1938, and reinstated on 1 May 1940. All of the aircraft delivered to No 1 Sqn in October-November 1938 had Type B roundels, which lacked the yellow and white rings, so it seems likely that this anonymous Hurricane arrived on the unit as an attrition replacement sometime in late August or very early September 1939. The 'old' roundel was soon modified by an airman equipped with pots of red and blue insignia paint and a brush! No 1 Sqn's pre-war 'NA' code letters were not long for this world either . . .

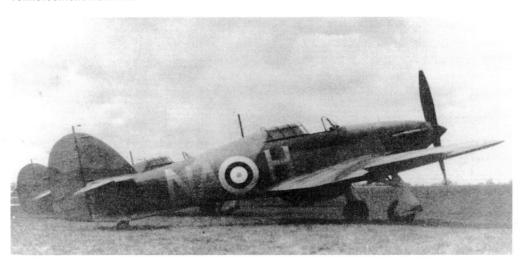

LEFT: . . . as this shot of a section of Hurricanes dispersed in a field 'somewhere in France' clearly shows. The 'JX' codes were applied literally days prior to the unit departing Tangmere for the continent on 8 September 1939. Pilots and groundcrews alike would share the tented accommodation

ABOVE: Conditions were far more civilised for the pilots when stood down, however. This group photograph was taken outside the mess at Pontavert, near the airfield at Berry-au-Bac, during the first week of May 1940. These individuals are, from left to right, Peter Boot, 'Hilly' Brown, F J Soper, Les Clisby (partly hidden), 'Pussy' Palmer, R L 'Lorry' Lorimer, 'Johnny' Walker and 'Killy' Kilmartin. Within days of this shot being taken the Germans had launched their invasion of the West, and the airfield had been abandoned in the face of the Blitzkrieg. Collectively, these pilots were responsible for downing a fair percentage of the 100+ German aircraft credited to No 1 Sqn whilst in France. Six of the eight pilots received decorations for their actions during this period, and Clisby and Lorimer were both killed in combat on 14 May.

Since 30 August, a Special Advanced Party of 16 Hurricanes had been at an hour's notice ready to deploy to France, the squadron receiving this instruction directly from the Air Ministry. The order also stated that the total support personnel to maintain the serviceablity of these fighters should not exceed 100 men, and that No 1 Sqn had to take 30 tons of stores with them so that they could remain in the field for at least a fortnight without having to be re-supplied.

In the wake of Prime Minister Chamberlain's announcement on the 3rd, No 1 Sqn's ground party had left for France, leaving the Hurricanes at Tangmere to be dispersed around the airfield, and the pilots and remaining groundcrew to move into tented accommodation whilst on standby. On the 7th, Sqn Ldr Halahan flew across to France to sort out billeting problems, and 24 hours later No 1 Sqn departed Tangmere for Le Havre's Octeville airfield. Fifteen Hurricanes made the short Channel crossing, although Plt Off 'Pussy' Palmer was not at the controls of one of them. He and four other pilots had been placed in charge of the ground party, and they proceeded to France by ship.

The arrival of No 1 Sqn on the continent marked the start of the RAF's build-up within the BEF, the air force's commitment to the expeditionary force being split into two elements. The first of these was the Advanced Air Striking Force (AASF), made up of Fairey Battle III medium bombers from Bomber Command's No 1 Group and, eventually, Blenheim IVs from No 2 Group. These squadrons were tasked primarily with strategic bombing operations, and initially had no

ABOVE: 'Pussy' Palmer and his section leader, Australian Flg Off Leslie Clisby, are seen at Vassincourt in the early spring of 1940. Both pilots had joined No 1 Sqn at around the same time, and would often fly together both in war and peace. A tough, no nonsense professional pilot, Les Clisby was officially credited with 16 and 1 shared destroyed by the time he was lost in action attacking a larger force of Bf 110s from 2./ZG 26 over Berry-au-Bac on the

LEFT: Dashing over the muddy expanses of Vassincourt towards their aircraft, pilots perform a mock scramble (note the smile on 'Lorry' Lorimer's face) for the benefit of the visiting press corps. This scene would be repeated three or four times a day following the launch of 'Operation Yellow' by the Germans in the early hours of 10 May. The pilots in this shot are, from left to right, Billy Drake, 'Lorry' Lorimer, 'Pussy' Palmer (in his pre-war 'prestige suit'), 'Prosser' Hanks and Les Clisby.

RIGHT: No 1 Sqn's L1679 was the regular mount of Flg Off Paul Richey for much of the 'Phoney War', although it was not one of the original 16 Hurricanes flown by the unit from Tangmere to Octeville on the morning of 8 September 1939. This fabric-winged, two-bladed Hurricane was, however, amongst the first batch of 14 Mk Is delivered to No 1 Sqn at Tangmere from the Hawker factory in October 1938. The exact date of its transfer to the continent is unknown, but Richey used the fighter to claim a third of a kill against a Do 17Z of 7./KG 3 on the opening day of the Blitzkrieg, followed by an unconfirmed victory against a second Dornier bomber (a Do 17P from 3.(F)/10) the following day. At the end of the latter combat Richey was forced to recover at the bombed-out airfield at Meziéres due to a shortage of fuel, and during his landing roll he swerved to miss a crater and dug L1679's port wing in – Richey abandoned the fighter and returned to his unit. Three days later a party of No 1 Sqn riggers was despatched to Meziéres to patch the aircraft up, but within minutes of their arrival the airfield was attacked, and the Hurricane (along with the 15 French Potez Po 63s based at the site) was summarily strafed for two-and-a-half hours by marauding Do 17s. Paul Richey described how he felt upon hearing the news in 'Fighter Pilot' – 'poor old "G" was sieved with bullets. I can only hope she burned before the Huns laid their rude hands on her'.

dedicated fighter cover from Fighter Command – the French air force was responsible for protecting AASF assets.

The second element – which was to operate closely with the ground forces of the BEF – was comprised of No 22 (Army Co-operation) Group in its entirety, plus a quartet of Hurricane I squadrons and two ex-No 1 Group Blenheim I units. Emphasising their close-support mission, the bulk of the squadrons assigned to No 22 Group flew Lysander IIs.

The four Hurricane units sent across the Channel were Nos 1, 73, 85 and 87 Sqns, and upon their arrival between 8 and 15 September, they became part of No 60 (Fighter) Wing. The fighter squadrons had been the first units within the Air Component despatched to France in order to cover the disembarkation of the ground troops, and their equipment.

Once the BEF had been safely put ashore, No 60 Wing's quartet of squadrons commenced their assigned role within the Air Component. However, following a series of losses to the Battle force during armed reconnaissance missions into Germany during late September, senior air force commanders within the BEF realised that the medium bombers of the AASF could not operate independently of dedicated RAF fighter escorts over enemy territory – their promised French fighter escorts had not proven up to the job.

Consequently, on 10 October Nos 1 and 73 Sqns were transferred from the Air Component to the AASF, forming No 67 (Fighter) Wing. Pilots within both units were extremely happy to hear this news, for they had quickly become bored of performing convoy patrols in between the spells of bad weather that signalled the imminent arrival of winter. No 1 Sqn moved to Vassincourt, some 50 miles east of Reims, whilst No 73 Sqn went to Rouvres, which was closer to the German border – No 1 Sqn would regularly send flights up to Rouvres on temporary detachment.

Throughout this period of mundane patrols, bad weather and base moving, 'Pussy' Palmer had gone about his business in much the same way as his fellow Hurricane pilots. Part of 'A' Flight's Red Section, he regularly flew patrols with his flight commander, 'Johnny' Walker, and veteran pre-war No 1 Sqn pilot, Sgt Francis Soper (who had scored 10 and 4 shared victories by the time he was posted missing in action in October 1941). And like all other fighter pilots in France, Palmer had not yet seen any action, although this was about to change.

On 30 October the fighter force at last encountered the enemy over France, Plt Off P W O 'Boy' Mould of No 1 Sqn's 'B' Flight downing a Do 17P of 2.(F)/123 that had been sent to photograph various French airfields near the German border. Due to poor weather and near incessant rain, another three weeks would pass before No 1 Sqn encountered the enemy once again. This time 'Pussy' Palmer was very much in the thick of the action, as two Do 17Ps and a solitary He 111K were all shot down on 23 November whilst on reconnaissance flights.

The first aircraft destroyed was a Dornier of 4.(F)/122, which force-landed near Moiremont, west of Verdun, at 11.00 hrs after being intercepted at 20,000 ft by 'A' Flight's Red Section. Leading the No 1 Sqn Hurricanes during the engagement was Plt Off 'Pussy' Palmer, and he and fellow section members Flg Off J I 'Killy' Kilmartin (who survived the war with a score of 12 or 13 destroyed, 2 shared destroyed and 1 damaged) and Sgt Soper were each credited with a third of a victory.

" 'Pussy' undid his straps and prepared to bail out …"

PAUL RICHEY

No 1 Sqn's Plt Off Paul Richey (a future ace with 10 and 1 shared kills) was serving as the unit's duty pilot in the operations room at Vassincourt on 23 November 1939, and in this extract from his famous wartime volume, *Fighter Pilot*, he recounts 'Pussy' Palmer's first action:

'A section from "A" Flight led by "Pussy" Palmer attacked the Dornier about 20 miles north of the airfield. "Pussy" led from dead astern. By the time he had used all his ammunition the rear-gunner and navigator had escaped by parachute and an engine was burning merrily. The Dornier was losing height and seemed to be more or less out of control. "Pussy" flew alongside the German aircraft to make sure the pilot was dead. He saw him slumped in his seat, his head lolling sideways. But suddenly the Dornier throttled back, swerved onto "Pussy's" tail as he overshot and put exactly 34 bullets through his Hurricane. Hearing them rip through, "Pussy" ducked and pushed the stick forward – thereby saving his life, as a bullet penetrated the locker behind his head and smashed the windscreen.

'Clouds of white smoke (which proved to be glycol) poured from the engine, which stopped. "Pussy" undid his straps and prepared to bail out, but the smoke stopped – presumably the glycol had finished – so he strapped up again and crash-landed safely with his undercarriage retracted. Meanwhile. "Killy" and Soper, number 2 and 3 of "Pussy's" section, attacked the Hun. With both engines now on fire, he crash-landed miraculously more or less in one piece. "Killy" and Soper circled and saw him wave as they passed low overhead. They returned to Vassincourt and "Pussy" was picked up by car.

'"Pussy's" combat with the Dornier had an important sequel that was to save the lives of many RAF fighter pilots. At this time the only armour our fighters carried was a thick cowling over the front petrol tank and a bullet-proof windscreen, while our Battles had thick armour plating behind the pilot – as indeed did the German fighters. After "Pussy's" lucky escape we decided we should have back armour too, and we asked for it.'

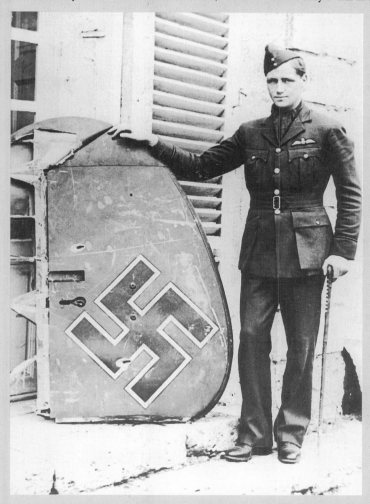

ABOVE: Flg Off Paul Richey kept a detailed diary of events pertaining to No 1 Sqn during its time in France, and he too flew with 'Pussy' Palmer on numerous occasions. Claiming eight and one shared destroyed during the Blitzkrieg, he was shot down and badly wounded on 19 May after despatching three He 111s in a matter of minutes. Following a spell in the American Hospital in Paris, Richey is seen here posing with the fin of a Bf 110 at Chateaudun on 14 June 1940 – he presented this 'trophy' to the unit following No 1 Sqn's epic engagement with I./ZG 26 on 11 May. In Richey's left hand is his 'shooting' stick, with nine notches carved into it to denote his victories. Within hours of this photograph being taken, Richey had been flown back to England in a de Havilland Rapide communications biplane chocked full of mail.

ABOVE: Having survived 13 days of near-constant combat, 'Pussy' Palmer, along with most of the surviving 'Phoney War' pilots in No 1 Sqn, was posted back to England on 23 May 1940. The following month he was one of ten pilots from the unit awarded the DFC (three sergeant pilots received DFMs at the same time) for his actions in France. By then he was commanding 'C' Flight of No 6 Operational Training Unit at Sutton Bridge. Remaining in Training Command until the autumn of 1942, Palmer was promoted to squadron leader and posted as a supernumerary to No 234 Sqn on 6 October. Flying Spitfire VBs from Portreath, on the north coast of Cornwall, he had completed just a handful of sweeps over France when he was reported missing in action in BH527 on 27 October. One of two pilots shot down when No 234 Sqn was 'bounced' by Fw 190s over Il de Batz, on the French coast, Palmer was seen to bale out but his body was never found.

The following month western Europe fell into the grip of one of the worst winters of the 20th century, grounding almost all aircraft on both sides of the Maginot Line. This meant a return to the 'Phoney War' for No 1 Sqn until things began to slowly 'thaw' in late February 1940.

Biggin Hill's First Kill

Forty-eight hours prior to 'Pussy' Palmer firing his first shots in anger, No 79 Sqn's Flg Off James Davies had played a key role in securing No 11 Group's second victory of World War 2 (its first kill had been claimed off Southend just the day before by a trio of Spitfires from No 74 Sqn).

Like all other Fighter Command units in the south-east of England, No 79 Sqn at Biggin Hill had failed to encounter the enemy during the first 11 weeks of war. It had, however, flown countless patrols over the Channel, and investigated numerous 'X' raids – all unidentified aircraft appearing on the Operations Room plotting table were so labelled. With the RAF convinced that German bombers would hit the south-east at anytime, and bombers already attacking naval targets in Scotland and northern England, fighter controllers left nothing to chance, as the following extract from Graham Wallace's volume *RAF Biggin Hill* clearly reveals:

'09.45 Blue Flight, 79 Sq. ordered to intercept doubtful raid No. X 42. No result.
'11.38 Yellow Section, 79 Sq. ordered to investigate with caution raid No. X 39. No result.
'12.19 Red Section, 79 Sq. ordered to investigate raid No. X 44. No result.
'12.56 Red Section, 79 Sq. ordered to investigate raid No. X 40. No result.'

Indeed, the only time that pilots from Biggin Hill had succeeded in firing their guns during the damp and cloudy autumn of 1939 was when called upon to destroy errant barrage balloons that had broken free from their moorings! This would all change on the morning of 21 November. Graham Wallace again:

RIGHT: By late 1939 both No 67 Wing fighter units had painted their Hurricanes in near-identical schemes, having forsaken distinguishing two-letter codes ('JX' for No 1 Sqn and 'TP' for No 73) for a single letter. This change was made to avoid confusion amongst the many French squadrons operating in this area – local pilots were not familiar with the RAF's code system. Improved identification was also the driving force behind the adoption of the non-standard red white and blue rudder, as several pilots within No 67 Wing were attacked by French fighters soon after moving into north-eastern France. This photograph perfectly illustrates the unique markings employed by Nos 1 and 73 Sqns, the latter unit's 'S for Sugar' being captured in the final moments of its approach to Rouvres in early December 1939.

'It fell to 79 Squadron to make Biggin Hill's first "kill" of the war. At 10 am on 21st November Yellow Section was ordered to patrol Hawkinge, the forward airfield of the sector. Only two Hurricanes took-off as the engine of the third failed to start. The pilots, Flying Officer Jimmy Davies, an amiable young American, and Flight Sergeant Brown, did not relish an hour's stooging up and down the South Coast in dirty weather. At 10.20 they were ordered to intercept an "X" raid over Dover. It was an Anson of Coastal Command. Then the vectors came thick and fast: at 10.31 back at Hawkinge at 12,000 feet; 10.38 Dover at 15,000 feet; 10.41 the South Foreland. The radio-location operators had a blip on their screens that could only be an enemy aircraft.

'There was a hint of excitement in the Controller's voice: "Hullo, Pansy (No 79 Sqn's code name) Yellow Leader. Sapper control. Vector 115 degrees, Angels 15 Buster!"

'The two Hurricanes swung onto the new course. Davies and Brown switched on their gun sights and twisted the safety-rings from "safe" to "fire". At 10.55 they sighted their quarry: "flying pencil", the Dornier 17, making a weather reconnaissance over the Channel.

'"Tally ho!"

'The Operations Room staff smiled when they heard Davies's American stammer over the loudspeaker. One of the plotters quickly moved a little red sticker, symbolising the Hurricanes, next to the black, enemy, sticker on the vertical glass map of the sector.

'They had an advantage of 3,000 feet over the Dornier. Unseen, the two Hurricanes dived down and opened fire at 600 yards. Davies chortled with delight as he smelt the acrid cordite fumes seep into his cockpit and saw, for the first time in his life, what eight Browning guns did to an enemy aircraft. Pieces flew off in all directions. With one engine streaming black smoke, the Dornier twisted over and spun into the clouds. Davies and Brown dived after it and emerged from the overcast to see it hit the sea with a wholly satisfying explosion.'

The aircraft destroyed by 'Jimmy' Davies and Flt Sgt Frederick Brown was one of two Do 17Ps sortied by 3.(F)/122, based at Goslar, south-east of Hannover. The long-range reconnaissance aircraft had been ordered to patrol up and down the Channel, probing Fighter Command's defences in order to gauge the effectiveness of the south coast RDF chain, as well as seeking out any notable shipping movements. The second Dornier made the long flight back to central Germany alone.

The Borkum Raid

Since the declaration of war in early September, No 79 Sqn had been sharing its Biggin Hill base with No 601 'County of London' Sqn, which had flown in from RAF Hendon on the 2nd. The auxiliary unit had undertaken a similar deployment during the Munich Crisis of September 1938, although this time No 601 Sqn was equipped with the Blenheim IF rather than the thoroughly obsolete Demon biplane fighter.

Amongst the crews sent to Kent were two American pilots, Flg Offs Carl Davis and Whitney Straight. Both were veteran pilots, having been with the unit since 1936 and 1937 respectively, and they now itched for an opportunity to engage the enemy. Being an accomplished aircraft

ABOVE: Taken at the same time as the previous photograph, this shot shows a No 73 Sqn two-bladed Hurricane I being started for the camera at Rouvres. The airmen with the cranking handles on either side of the fighter are Leading Aircraftsmen W 'Gooney' Slater and Dave Dalziel, the pilot is New Zealander Plt Off Bill Kain and the 'Chiefy' with his thumbs up is Sgt Hughie Gallagher. Note the fighter's split 'Night and White' undersides.

LEFT: Re-arming and refuelling fighters in the field in France became progressively more difficult as the Germans thrust towards the Channel at great speed. Even prior to the *Blitzkrieg*, turning fighters around on the ground was a labour-intensive task, as this shot of a No 1 Sqn Hurricane in early 1940 clearly shows. Lacking a three-point Albion bowser from which to refuel, groundcrews are having to make do with a small wheeled cart, alongside which are boxes of ammunition. An armourer can be seen tending the port quartet of 0.303-in Browning guns, and at the extreme right of the photograph a pilot chats with his 'Chiefy'. This shot was almost certainly taken pre-*Blitzkrieg*, for only one member of the groundcrew is wearing a steel helmet.

designer, Straight, in particular, looked at ways of improving his Blenheim to increase his chances of survival should he enter combat. One area that particularly concerned him was the aircraft's total lack of armour plating for the crew, so he ordered some armoured seats on his own account with the Wilkinson Sword Company. These were duly fitted, as was additional armour plating that he acquired privately from the aircraft's manufacturer! The latter shifted the Blenheim's centre of gravity and made the aircraft difficult to fly, so it had to be removed.

Like the other fighter units based at Biggin Hill, No 601 Sqn spent most of the 'Phoney War' intercepting 'X' raids. However, on 27 November the unit was tasked with performing a daring daylight raid on the seaplane base at Borkum, on the Friesian Island of Sylt off the German North Sea coast. Floatplanes and flying boats of the *Küstenfliegergruppen* had been laying magnetic mines in British waters, and these had caused grave losses to both naval vessels and merchant ships alike.

Six of the most experienced pilots in the squadron – including Carl Davis – were chosen for the long-range mission, which would see British fighters cross into German territory for the first time. No 601 Sqn's Blenheims were split into two sections, one of which was led by Flg Off Max Aitken:

'In addition to the six aircraft from 601 Squadron, there were six from 25 Squadron. We were not allowed to carry any bombs; we flew from Biggin Hill to Northolt where we had a conference with Orlebar (the Station Commander) who told us: "You are lucky to have a first crack at the enemy". I am not sure whether we saw it quite in this light. We stopped for lunch at Bircham Newton but, curiously, none of us was inclined to eat. After flying over the North Sea for half an hour, we were fired at by one of our convoys, but continued flying along the Dutch coast to Borkum, which we approached very low. It was my job to deal with the German fighters. After that we turned towards the seaplane base. I have a vivid recollection of the attack. I saw a man standing on a ladder painting one of the hangars. He fell off the ladder. His hat fell off with him. So far as I know that was all the damage we did at Borkum that day.

'Flying home again, we were once more fired on by our own convoy. By the time we reached the English coast it was dark. We had no wireless. The balloon barrage which might have made things awkward was up, but the Station Commander at Debden had the good sense to turn on a searchlight which he pointed straight up in the air as a beacon. All the aircraft made for it, as a result of which there were a great many near misses. I was the last to land, very short of petrol. We had encountered a great deal of anti-aircraft fire but fortunately no German fighters. On the following day we were back at home at Biggin Hill, and to celebrate our safe return the Station Commander renamed his house Borkum.'

No 601 Sqn would not encounter the enemy again until the middle of May 1940, by which time the unit had swapped its Blenheim IFs for Hurricane Is.

LEFT: All aircraft maintenance in France took place in the open, as this photograph of No 1 Sqn's 'S' clearly shows. With the groundcrew off having a tea break, the fighter is left sitting on jacks awaiting an engine change. A factory-fresh Rolls-Royce Merlin II, unsoiled by glycol leaks or oil smears, sits in its packing crate ready for fitting. This photo was taken at Vassincourt in March 1940.

RIGHT: More heavy maintenance at Vassincourt. The airmen have enlisted the support of a mobile crane on this occasion, rather than relying on a block and tackle. The Hurricane's poorly placed reserve fuel tank, immediately forward of the cockpit, can be clearly seen in this photograph. On 2 April 1940, 'Pussy' Palmer's aircraft sustained a hit in the reserve tank when he was bounced by Bf 109s near Saarbrucken. His fighter caught fire and he was forced to bail out (see page 22).

Fighters

With the improvement of the weather on the continent by March 1940, RAF fighters within No 67 Wing began to encounter German reconnaissance aircraft with a growing frequency. These aircraft usually ventured into northern France without a fighter escort, although by late March examples of both the twin-engined Messerschmitt Bf 110 *Zerstörer* and the single-engined Bf 109E had been intercepted by Hurricane pilots. Indeed, the first action which pitted No 1 Sqn against the *Emil* involved 'Pussy' Palmer, for on 29 March he was leading a section on a patrol over Metz when two Bf 109Es of III./JG 53 were spotted at 25,000 ft.

ABOVE: A number of Hurricane Is issued to No 1 Sqn were eventually passed to No 73 Sqn as the former unit received newer aircraft fitted with variable pitch propellers in late 1939 – N2358 was one such machine. Coded 'Z' by No 1 Sqn soon after its arrival at Vassincourt in November 1939 (following brief service with No 43 Sqn at Acklington), the fighter retained this marking when it was passed on to No 73 Sqn at Rouvres early in the New Year. Parked in No 1 Sqn's muddy dispersal area on the edge of Vassincourt airfield, the fighter is being refuelled from the unit's Albion three-point bowser whilst its fitter tinkers with the engine. N2358 was one of twelve Hurricanes hastily plucked out of the frontline, or from maintenance units, and sent to Glosters for refurbishment, prior to being shipped to Finland in late February 1940 for service with the Finnish air force.

Just as the Hurricanes closed on the first German fighters encountered by No 1 Sqn, Plt Off 'Pete' Matthews, flying as 'No 3' in the section, believed he saw a further trio of *Emils* diving on them and he immediately called '*Look out behind!*'. Palmer broke hard to port – too hard, for his Hurricane spun down out of control, the pilot levelling out at 10,000 ft. Matthews had also performed a violent evasive manoeuvre, blacking out in the process and only coming to after losing some 15,000 ft in altitude! This left the third member of the section, Plt Off Paul Richey, to engage the Bf 109s on his own and he duly claimed No 1 Sqn's first victory over a fighter in the Second World War.

Further clashes with German fighters occurred over the following days and No 1 Sqn scored a handful of kills without suffering any losses. However, that changed on the morning of 2 April, when 'Pussy' Palmer fell victim to a surprise 'bounce' by Bf 109Es of III./JG 53. He subsequently described the action to Noel Monks, the war correspondent for *The Daily Mail*:

'I was a member of a flight of five Hurricanes led by Flg Off Clisby. At 11 am over Metz we sighted some enemy aircraft above us. We chased after them, going eastward. Near Saarbrucken I saw five Me 109s above and behind us. I called Clisby over the phone but this failed to attract him because someone else was switched on to "send". I flew past him and turned towards the enemy aircraft. I had been ordered to guard our tails and I turned from side to side so as I could keep a lookout astern, before following after the rest of the flight. Once, as I looked behind I saw two Messerschmitts diving on my tail. I called over the radio: "Ware enemy aircraft", and took avoiding action, but a shell burst in my reserve petrol tank setting it on fire. Flames entered the cockpit. I was now at about 22,000 ft and I turned the aircraft over on its back, opened the hood and released my harness as I pushed the stick hard forward. I left the cockpit safely and opened the parachute after a delayed drop of 5000 ft in order to avoid the combat that had broken out above me.

'I landed in a tree in a wood 500 yards from the German lines, and when I climbed down I jumped into the arms of a French patrol who took me back to their lines.

'I returned to my unit the next day.'

The pilot that had set Palmer's Hurricane (N2326) aflame was none other than *Hptm.* Werner Mölders, who had claimed 14 victories during the Spanish Civil War and seven to date during the 'Phoney War'. Seemingly unruffled by his brush with death, the chain-smoking Palmer had enjoyed a cigarette whilst taking in the view during his long descent!

Blitzkrieg

The 'Phoney War' came to an end in the early hours of 10 May 1940, when the Germans instigated Operation *Yellow* – the invasion of Belgium, Holland and France by land and air. Although No 1 Sqn was already in northern France at the time of the invasion, it was actually

Hawker Hurricane I N2358 of No 1 Sqn, Vassincourt, November 1939
Fitted with a three-bladed variable pitch de Havilland propeller, N2358 was one of a
handful of near new Hurricanes issued to No 1 Sqn in late 1939 as replacements for the
unit's original two-bladed machines. It was flown several times by Flg Off 'Pussy' Palmer
prior to being passed on to No 73 Sqn in early 1940.

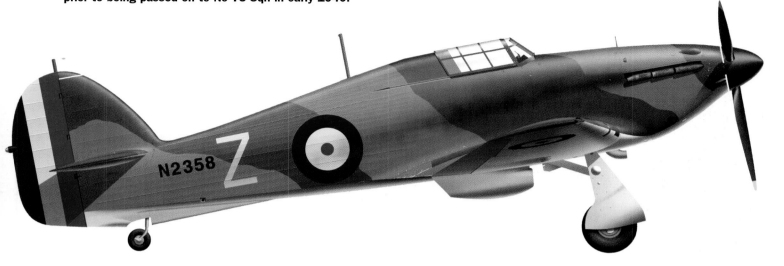

Flg Off 'Jimmy' Davies of No 79 Sqn who claimed the first kill for the American contingent during
the Battle of France.

Within hours of Operation *Yellow* commencing, the Biggin Hill-based unit had been one of
four Hurricane squadrons sent to France as reinforcements for the BEF. These units had in fact
been originally scheduled to deploy to the continent weeks earlier, but the Air Staff had argued
that commitments elsewhere (in Norway and northern Britain) took precedence at the time.

Assigned to the Air Component's No 63 Wing, No 79 Sqn arrived at Merville, west of Lille,
in the early afternoon of 10 May, and the unit was soon aloft once again on its first patrol from
its new base. The Luftwaffe was nowhere to be seen, however, and it was not until the following
morning that No 79 Sqn engaged the enemy, downing a single He 111H of *Stab./KG* 1. The
bombers had offered stiff resistance, destroying two Hurricanes – one pilot escaped unscathed
whilst the second suffered badly burnt arms. The latter individual was 'A' Flight Commander, Flt
Lt Bob Edwards, and his position was quickly filled by 'Jimmy' Davies.

With No 79 Sqn's CO struck down by illness soon after the unit arrived in France, Flg Off
Davies now effectively led the squadron whenever it was airborne. He would set a fine example
for his men during the subsequent weeks of near-constant action, scoring his first victories of
the campaign late on the afternoon of 12 May when he claimed a He 111 destroyed and a

RIGHT: The AASF's most successful fighter
squadron during the Battle of France (10 to 21
May), No 1 Sqn was credited with 63 kills
confirmed and 11 probables, for the loss of two
pilots killed, one captured and four wounded. The
unit also suffered heavily with 21 Hurricanes
destroyed, the bulk of which were abandoned on
the ground. Of the 22 units to see action during the
Blitzkrieg, only the Air Component's Nos 3 and 85
Sqns, with 67 and 64.5 kills respectively, outscored
No 1 Sqn. In this famous press photograph, the
officers of No 1 Sqn pose for one final group shot
outside their hotel (the 'Mairie') at Neuville in early
1940. They are, from left to right, Plt Off Billy Drake,
Flg Offs Les Clisby and 'Lorry' Lorimer (both killed
in action on 14 May 1940), Flt Lt 'Prosser' Hanks, Plt
Off 'Boy' Mould, Sqn Ldr 'Bull' Halahan, Lt 'Moses'
Demozay (French liaison officer), Flt Lt 'Johnny'
Walker, 'Doc' Brown (squadron medical officer), Flg
Offs Paul Richey and 'Killy' Kilmartin, Plt Off J S
Mitchell (killed in action on 2 March 1940) and Flg
Off 'Pussy' Palmer. Note that both Walker and Palmer
are wearing carpet slippers!

second Heinkel as a probable. That same day No 79 Sqn moved further west to Norrent-Fontes.

On 14 May both 'Pussy' Palmer and 'Jimmy' Davies were credited with kills, as the RAF contingent in France launched its sole co-ordinated attack on the advancing Germany army. The fighter units in-theatre were given the task of escorting Battles and Blenheims as they attempted to knock out pontoon bridges spanning the river Meuse, and thus stall the advance of the all-conquering *Panzers*. No 1 Sqn engaged a formation of unescorted Ju 87 Stukas of 2./StG 77 whilst in the vicinity of the Allied bombers, and swiftly shot five of them down. The Hurricane pilots then bounced the Bf 109Es of I./JG 53 that were supposedly escorting the Ju 87s, claiming four destroyed in quick succession – one of these fell to 'Pussy' Palmer.

On the final bridge raid of the day, five No 79 Sqn Hurricanes were the only escorts available for the 28 Blenheims sent against targets in the Bouillon-Givonne-Sedan region. The promised escort of 18 fighters was to include Hurricanes from both Nos 1 and 73 Sqns, but these units had suffered six losses between them earlier in the day.

Leading the No 79 Sqn aircraft was 'Jimmy' Davies in L2140, whilst his counterpart in the Blenheim formation was Wg Cdr Basil Embry, CO of No 107 Sqn. The latter pilot later wrote in his autobiography, *Mission Completed*:

'About 40 miles from the target I saw flying below and to the side a German light reconnaissance aeroplane, and attracted Whiting's (Sgt Tom Whiting, navigator) attention to it. As I did so a section of Hurricanes dived, firing their guns, and in a minute it just disintegrated. Someone described it later as "bursting like a light bulb".'

The Henschel Hs 126 army co-operation aircraft had fallen victim to Flg Off Davies. Minutes later No 79 Sqn encountered a far deadlier foe – 15 Bf 110Cs of ZG 1. Although outnumbered, the Hurricane pilots engaged their German counterparts at an altitude of 6,000 ft north of the French town of Leuze. No 79 Sqn's Plt Off John Wood was soon forced to abandon his shot up Hurricane, but 'Jimmy' Davies evened the score when he claimed a Bf 110 destroyed.

Neither Davies or Palmer added to their tallies over the next 48 hours, although both men experienced base moves with their respective units as the Germans pushed further westward into France. By now the situation was becoming grave. Units were seriously depleted, with losses of both men and machinery not being replaced, the French army was in headlong retreat, the shattered remnants of the BEF were conducting a 'fighting withdrawal' through northern France, and the *Luftwaffe* had all but won control of the skies.

No 1 Sqn had been moved to Conde/Vraux, mid-way between Reims and Paris, just after dawn on 17 May, and although short on fuel, ammunition and groundcrew, acting CO, Flt Lt 'Johnny' Walker, led 'A' Flight aloft at 09.00 hrs following reports of German dive-bombers attacking Allied troops near Sedan. No Ju 87s were found, although around 25 Bf 110Cs of V.(Z)/LG 1 were spotted near Vouziers. Climbing to 18,000 ft, the five Hurricane pilots then dived on the Messerschmitt fighters. In the ensuing battle, No 1 Sqn pilots claimed six Bf 110s destroyed, but in reality V.(Z)/LG 1 had lost half this number. Although not directly involved in this sortie, Paul Richey vividly recounted the epic dogfight in *Fighter Pilot*:

'Soon all the Flight came trickling back. Johnny, Hilly and Killy had each shot down a 110, and Soper two. 'Pussy' was missing. He was missing all morning. When this happened we ignored it, didn't even mention the name. It wasn't a conscious effort at tact – we no longer knew the meaning of the word – but an automatic reticence, a reluctance to discuss possibilities of which each one of us was only too well aware.

'And 'Pussy' turned up all right, as most of us had. He had shot down a 110, gone down in flames himself (in P2820) and bailed out. This was his second bail-out, and the French had taken advantage of the situation by using him for target practice as he floated down. They invariably assumed that anyone in a parachute was automatically a Hun. 'Pussy' was greatly discomforted as some 30 rifle shots whined past him, but when he hit the ground he turned his excellent command of the more colourful side of the French language to good account. His eloquence even surprised the soldiers!'

Having survived being shot down twice, as well as force-landing a badly damaged fighter, Flg Off Cyril Dampier 'Pussy' Palmer was living on borrowed time. His CO, 'Bull' Halahan, recognised this fact, and on

BELOW: Late in the morning of 23 November 1939, 'Pussy' Palmer's 'A' Section succeeded in destroying a Do 17P of 4.(F)/122, which force-landed near Moiremont, west of Verdun, after being intercepted at 20,000 ft. During the course of the action Palmer himself was almost shot down when the Dornier's pilot, Unteroffizier Arno Frankenburger, succeeded in hitting the American's Hurricane with 34 rounds. The German was captured by French troops after crash-landing his stricken reconnaissance bomber, and he was later entertained in No 1 Sqn's Officers' Mess at Neuville. Prior to being packed off to a PoW camp, Frankenburger presented his hosts with this photograph of himself, on the back of which he had inscribed, 'With eternal thanks on the part of a vanquished Arno Frankenburger – What a pity – A.F.'

on 17 May he duly sent a request to his superiors in No 67 Wing that those pilots still with the squadron who had been in France since September be returned to England immediately. Six days later Halahan, his flight commanders and six pilots (including 'Pussy' Palmer) departed France for England.

There would be no such respite for 'Jimmy' Davies and the now seriously depleted No 79 Sqn. The day after escorting the Blenheims sent to attack the bridges at Sedan, the unit had returned to Merville, and on the morning of the 18th Davies was in the thick of the action once again. This time he destroyed a Do 17Z of 5./KG 76 that was part of a formation that overflew No 79 Sqn's airfield at low-level. This would be the American's final kill during the Battle of France, for on 20 May his squadron flew its few remaining Hurricanes directly back to Biggin Hill from Merville.

In just ten days of near-constant combat, No 79 Sqn had lost ten Hurricanes, although only five of these had been destroyed by enemy action. Two pilots had been killed, one made a prisoner of war and two wounded. In return, the unit had claimed 23.25 German aircraft destroyed, of which 'Jimmy' Davies had been credited with downing four and one probable.

Of the quartet of Americans serving with Fighter Command during the Battle of France, it appears that only J W E Davies and C D Palmer saw actual combat. No 601 Sqn's Flg Off Whitney Straight had been posted to Norway in late April on a special assignment as part of the RAF's contribution to the ill-fated defence of Scandinavia, whilst his squadronmate, Carl Davis, had remained at Tangmere with 'B' Flight when 'A' Flight had been posted to France on 16 May.

Operation *Dynamo*

With both the French and British armies now thoroughly routed, and columns of troops retreating into north-western France, the RAF pulled the bulk of its surviving fighter force back across the Channel. These battle-weary units would have little time to rest and re-group, however, for they would now be needed to protect the mass evacuation of the BEF from Dunkirk.

Codenamed Operation *Dynamo*, the evacuation proper began on 26 May when the Admiralty sent the first vessels into the bomb-damaged harbour at the French sea port to pick up British troops. Over the next nine days more than 338,000 virtually weaponless 'Tommies' were saved from certain capture.

The units within Fighter Command committed to this daring operation were ordered to '*Ensure the protection of the Dunkirk beaches (three miles on either side of the town) from first*

ABOVE: Like most units that were rushed to France in the wake of 'Operation Yellow', No 79 Sqn was rarely photographed whilst on the continent. This priceless view, which was taken on the day of the invasion – 10 May 1940 – at Merville, shows Plt Offs Lou Appleton (killed on 14 May), J E R Wood (killed on 8 July), 'Dimsie' Stones and American 'Jimmy' Davies soon after they had arrived in France. Their French counter-parts, and the Morane MS.406 fighters behind them, belonged to the Merville-based 2eme Escadrille of GC III/1. This is the only wartime shot of 'Jimmy' Davies that has come to the author's attention, and the original is held in the collection of 'Dimsie' Stones.

LEFT: Very few photographs exist of No 601 Sqn's Blenheim IFs, this rare view showing three examples 'on the wing' from Biggin Hill soon after the unit was mobilised following the declaration of war on 3 September 1939. The aircraft in the foreground was being flown by Flt Lt Roger Bushell when this shot was taken. A pre-war pilot, who was subsequently downed over Dunkirk in late May 1940 whilst flying a Spitfire as CO of No 92 Sqn, Bushell became a Prisoner of War (PoW). He later gained fame as 'Big X' at Sagan camp when he led the 'Great Escape' of March 1944, and was one of 50 RAF officers to be murdered by the Germans following recapture.

light to darkness by continuous fighter patrols in strength'. Opposing Fighter Command was the might of the all-conquering *Luftwaffe*, which had been given the task of foiling any rescue attempt by the Royal Navy.

Dynamo was an almost exclusively No 11 Group affair for Fighter Command, with 14 Hurricane and 13 Spitfire units seeing action over Dunkirk. One of those units involved was No 79 Sqn, although due to a dearth of both men and machinery its participation lasted just 24 hours. Having returned to Biggin Hill on 21 May, the unit had been able to cobble together a handful of airworthy Hurricanes by the time *Dynamo* commenced. Having to rely on groundcrews borrowed from other units at the station (Nos 32, 213 and 242 Sqns), No 79 Sqn was still non-operational for the first 24 hours of the evacuation, but on the evening of the 27th it succeeded in putting up six aircraft in the form of 'A' Flight, led by Flg Off 'Jimmy' Davies.

Amongst the Battle of France survivors who participated in this mission was Plt Off D W A 'Dimsie' Stones, who, like his flight commander, had enjoyed success during the *Blitzkrieg*. In this extract taken from his autobiography, *Dimsie*, Stones describes this memorable sortie over the evacuation beaches;

'Our section of "A" Flight patrolled Gravelines (west of Dunkirk) to Veurne (just inland from the Belgian coast) during the Dunkirk evacuation and ran into a formation of Me 110s. One attacked Jimmy, but overshot him and turned in front of me. I was lucky with my first burst and hit one of his engines and maybe the cockpit. He dived steeply to the sea past Jimmy, who also got in a burst, and later confirmed that it hit the sea whilst I was engaging another Me 110. We

Bristol Blenheim IF (serial unknown) of No 601 'County of London' Sqn, Tangmere, November 1939
Operated by a handful of Fighter Command units as a 'heavy' fighter, this Blenheim IF was flown by a number of pilots during its time with No 601 Sqn, including flight commander Flt Lt Roger Bushell and American Flg Off Carl Davis.

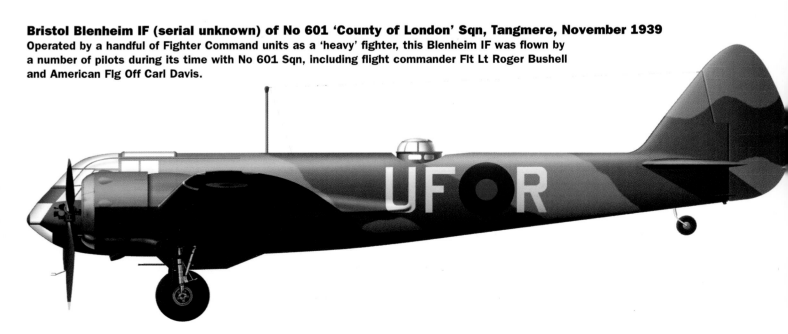

LEFT: In early December 1939 No 601 Sqn moved south from Biggin Hill to Tangmere, where this photograph was taken on what appears to be a less than ideal day for flying. Note that the fuselage roundel has been changed from a Munich Crisis style Type B of blue and red to a Type A, which was officially authorised on 21 November 1939. The aircraft's Medium Sea Grey codes also appear to have been applied in a much lighter shade than on Roger Bushell's 'UF-R', seen opposite.

filled in out combat reports at base and I suggested we should share the Me 110 which went into the sea. Jimmy would have none of it, insisting that it was on its way in before he fired, and gave me credit for it. That is what a generous fighter pilot Jimmy was.'

Upon returning to Biggin Hill, Davies and Stones each claimed one Bf 110 destroyed, as well as one probable and one unconfirmed destroyed respectively. These aircraft were almost certainly from I./ZG 52, which lost three Bf 110s in combat with RAF fighters on this day. These kills made both 'Jimmy' Davies and 'Dimsie' Stones aces, each pilot have achieved the requisite five victories in order to be accorded such an accolade. It is unlikely that any great fuss was made by either individual upon attaining this distinction, and the following day No 79 Sqn was posted north to Digby, south of Lincoln, in order to rest and re-equip.

By the time the unit returned to Biggin Hill on 5 June *Dynamo* was over, and the bulk of the BEF – as well as 100,000+ French troops – had been returned to Britain. Having covered the evacuation as best it could, No 11 Group then switched to escorting Blenheim bombers flying sorties in support of the 160,000 British soldiers still in France fighting the Germans.

The first of these missions involving No 79 Sqn took place on the afternoon of 7 June, when it joined No 32 Sqn in providing the fighter escort for 30 Blenheims of No 2 Group's Nos 15, 107 and 110 Sqns. Sent to attack enemy troop convoys in the Abbeville area, this force was the largest of its kind despatched to France since *Dynamo* had ended.

The formation was attacked by around 40 Bf 109Es once over the target, and as per the mission brief at Biggin Hill, No 79 Sqn engaged the enemy fighters while No 32 remained with the bombers. In the bitter dogfight that ensued Hurricane pilots were credited with downing four *Emils*, with a further two being listed as probably destroyed. In a case of mistaken identity, 'Jimmy' Davies claimed a 'He 113' destroyed and a second unconfirmed destroyed. Thanks to an active propaganda campaign instigated by the *Luftwaffe*, the limited-production Heinkel fighter (designated the He 100 by the manufacturer) was regularly 'encountered' by the RAF during the summer of 1940, although only a handful were built, and these never saw action!

No Blenheims were lost on 7 June thanks to the effective escorting of the Biggin Hill 'wing'. The following morning both units were sent to patrol the coastline north and south of Le Tréport harbour in an effort to prevent German bombers from attacking the ongoing evacuation. Patrolling at 10,000 ft up and down the coast on a hot, sunny day, the Hurricane pilots saw nothing for the first 30 minutes of the mission, then No 32 Sqn spotted a large formation of unescorted He 111s heading for the French port. The unit quickly adopted a line astern formation in order to carry out a textbook attack.

Whilst '32nd Pursuit' mauled the bombers, No 79 Sqn engaged the Bf 109 escort that had arrived too late to protect the Heinkels. Fighting through the *Emils*, 'Jimmy' Davies and 'Dimsie' Stones succeeded in sharing in the destruction of a He 111, and upon returning to Biggin Hill they were notified that they had each been awarded the Distinguished Flying Cross (DFC).

For the remainder of the month the Biggin Hill squadrons flew their fair share of defensive sorties along the French coast, although little was achieved during the flights. One of the participants in these missions was No 32 Sqn flight commander Flt Lt P M 'Pete' Brothers, who was a close friend of 'Jimmy' Davies:

ABOVE: Buttoned up in his standard issue RAF greatcoat, and chewing on his trademark pipe, Flg Off Whitney Straight poses in front of his Blenheim IF at a snowy Tangmere in January 1940. He had this aircraft specially modified through the fitment of armoured seats purchased privately from Wilkinson Sword! Note the fighter's four-gun pack bolted under the bomb-bay, this fitment containing 2000 rounds of belted 0.303-in ammunition. More than 1,300 of these packs were constructed by Southern Railway's Ashford works in Kent.

'Jimmy was a gentleman, with a quiet charm and a kind, thoughtful and careful way. He had only a very slight American accent, so slight that my wife Annette, who knew him well, never realised that he was an American. Not being in the same squadron, we only met in the Mess, and although that was where the high jinks took place, I cannot remember him "stirring the pot" – he was too gentle. To sum up, I found him a truly delightful and trustworthy person. That's why he was invited to my wedding.'

Like many seasoned Fighter Command pilots, 'Pete' Brothers could not understand why good men and aircraft were being sacrificed in the pointless Channel patrols of June and early July 1940;

'After Dunkirk we were flying these utterly stupid patrols in wing strength to demonstrate air superiority. We would be detailed to fly down the French coast, cross in at Calais and then fly down to Amiens, before turning around and coming back. All of the Bf 109 chaps at Merville and Abbeville would simply rub there hands and say: "*Oh, there they go*", and then they would take-off just as we returned towards Calais. By this stage, invariably the sun was behind us and we would have to get home sharpish because we were by then short of fuel. They would then simply climb up and jump us. This happened time and time again, and we were getting hammered for no reason at all.'

Brothers' words proved truly prophetic, for on the morning of 27 June No 79 Sqn lost two pilots whilst off the French coast – one of them was 'Jimmy' Davies. The unit had been briefed to escort a flight of Blenheims on a photo-reconnaissance mission to St Valéry-en-Caux, just south of Dieppe, No 79 Sqn providing the top escort at 10,000 ft whilst two other units protected the front and rear of the formation. The enemy failed to react en route to the target, but once the Blenheims crossed the coast on their return flight, three Bf 109Es (from II./JG 51) were spotted diving out of the sun by No 79 Sqn's 'weaver', Plt Off Tom Parker. He immediately called his flight leader, now Flt Lt J W E Davies.

'*Hullo, Leader. Weaver calling. Bandits on our tail. LOOK OUT!*'

The formation failed to react, however, for Parker's radio transmitter had gone unserviceable. He watched in horror as the *Emils* fired mortal bursts into the aircraft of 'Jimmy' Davies and his wingman, Sgt R R McQueen. Both fighters belched out black smoke and fell away from the formation, whilst the Messerschmitt pilots effected their escape at full throttle. McQueen succeeded in bailing out of his blazing fighter, and he came down in the Channel. For the next 90 minutes a number of Hurricanes took it in turns to overfly the pilot as he remained afloat through his inflated 'Mae West' just off the French coast. To his colleagues flying above him, the sergeant pilot appeared to be uninjured, but when the Rye lifeboat reached McQueen he was dead.

BELOW LEFT: Heavy snowfall characterised the winter of 1939-40, and Tangmere was not spared despite its proximity to the sea. These No 601 Sqn Blenheim IFs were resident at the airfield throughout the harsh winter months, groundcrews struggling in the open to keep the fighters airworthy. Note that the 'UF' section of the code on the Blenheim in the foreground appears to have been applied in a much darker shade than its individual identification letter.

There was no sign of 'Jimmy' Davies, however, and his loss was keenly felt within No 79 Sqn. Plt Off D W A 'Dimsie' Stones summed up his fellow pilots' feelings in the following extract, taken from his autobiography:

'Jimmy made a splendid flight commander and I was glad to serve under him in "A" Flight until he was so tragically killed on 27 June. He had great charm, and was always cheerful and full of energy. His exuberance on the ground was described by all of us in one phrase: "Jimmy's Whizzing again!"'

No 79 Sqn would lose a further four pilots (including its CO) killed in action over the Channel up until 11 July, when the battle-weary unit was at last removed from No 11 Group and sent north to Acklington to re-group.

Of the four Americans within Fighter Command upon the declaration of war, only Flg Off Carl Davis remained in the frontline (at Tangmere with No 601 Sqn) come the eve of the Battle of Britain.

"At last only one Distinguished Flying Cross lay on the cushion..."

GRAHAM WALLACE

On the day Flt Lt J W E 'Jimmy' Davies was lost in action, he had been informed just prior to take-off that His Majesty King George VI would be visiting Biggin Hill to hold an investiture for those men that had been awarded medals for gallantry in the Dunkirk and French campaigns. The presentations would be made in the late morning, soon after No 79 Sqn had completed its mission to France. Graham Wallace described the scene in his volume *RAF Biggin Hill*:

'Biggin Hill was *en fete* for his Majesty. All the officers, airmen and WAAFs who could be spared from duty were on parade. Standing apart in a small, self-conscious group were the pilots waiting to be "gonged": the Distinguished Flying Cross for Flt Lt Crossley, Plt Offs Daw and Grice of 32 Squadron, and Plt Off Stones of 79 Squadron; the Distinguished Flying Medal for Sergeants Cartwright and Whitby. Each in turn marched smartly to the table where the King stood with Grp Capt Grice. They saluted and remained at attention while the citations were read:

"... *displayed great qualities of leadership ... exceptional courage and coolness ... devotion to duty ... complete disregard for his own personal safety ... excellent example to others ...*"

'The low-pitched, sentential phrases were belied by the sympathy and understanding in His Majesty's eyes.

'At last only one Distinguished Flying Cross lay on the cushion. It was to have been presented to Flt Lt Jimmy Davies of 79 Squadron. Since making Biggin Hill's first "kill", he had added five "certainties" to his score. His was the second of two Hurricanes shot down that morning. Right up to the end of the ceremony everyone hoped that he would reappear, smiling and nonchalantly apologising for being late on parade.'

LEFT: On the morning of 27 June 1940, His Majesty King George VI visited Biggin Hill to present DFCs and DFMs to pilots from Nos 32 and 79 Sqns following their acts of bravery over France. This photograph was taken during the investiture, which was held in front of the North Camps Belfast hangar – note the medals pinned to the chests of each of the pilots lined up in the foreground. Flt Lt Michael 'Red Knight' Crossley of No 32 Sqn is chatting with the King, whilst behind him, waiting their turn to talk with His Royal Highness, are Plt Offs V G 'Jack' Daw and D H 'Grubby' Grice, both from No 32 Sqn, and No 79 Sqn's Plt Off 'Dimsie' Stones and Sgts H Cartwright (killed in action exactly one week later) and A W Whitby. Flt Lt 'Jimmy' Davies was also due to receive his DFC at this ceremony, but he had been shot down and killed over the Channel on the very morning the investiture took place.

'Hack' Russell – Australian or American?

'I was searching the sky for him and momentarily drew abreast of Hack. In that precise moment an Me 110 must have crept up astern. I saw Hack, surrounded by bursting shells and tracer, pull up in a near-vertical climb, then fall off in a stall and commence a long slow spiral into the sea. I followed him down till it was obvious he was not in control, and then climbed hard. The Me 110 was still there, flying in a wide circle.'

This was how Flg Off A R 'Paul' Edge described the demise of his section leader, Flg Off I B N 'Hack' Russell, who was downed on the afternoon of 1 June 1940. Both men were assigned to Spitfire I-equipped No 609 'West Riding' Sqn, which was participating in Operation *Dynamo* from its base at RAF Northolt in Middlesex.

The exact nationality of 'Hack' Russell remains something of a mystery, for he is quoted in various works of reference as being both an Australian and an American! Born in the Australian city of Melbourne, in the state of Victoria, on 22 May 1911, Ian Bedford Nesbitt Russell joined the RAF on a short-service commission in 1936, having obtained a pilot's licence in April 1935. Following training with No 11 Flying Training School at RAF Wittering, Russell inexplicably resigned his commission and moved to the USA, where he flew airliners for a while.

Upon the outbreak of war he returned to the UK to re-enlist in the RAF, and by November 1939 Russell had been posted to the auxiliary-manned No 609 Sqn, based at Drem, east of Edinburgh. He was one of the first Regular pilots assigned to the unit, and is remembered in the following quote from *Under the White Rose*, written by No 609 Sqn's Intelligence Officer, Frank Ziegler:

'Flg Off I B N Russell was known to his fellow-officers as 'Hack', and to the ground staff as 'Hank'. Though he evidently felt the cold, and flew wrapped up like an Eskimo, he is described as "an unscareable tough guy" – an impression perhaps enhanced by the fact that he never stopped smoking while flying a Spitfire.'

Having seen no action with No 609 Sqn in Scotland, but having flown innumerable coastal convoy patrols and 'X' raid interceptions, 'Hack' Russell was posted to Hurricane-equipped No 245 Sqn on 8 May 1940. He did not have to move far, however, for his new unit was also based at Drem! Having barely had time to familiarise himself with the Hawker fighter's 'knobs and tits', Russell was despatched to France just five days after arriving on the squadron. With the *Blitzkrieg* in full swing, the Australian (along with a New Zealander from the same unit by the name of Plt Off J S 'Jim' Humphreys) was sent to No 607 'County of Durham' Sqn at Vitry-en-Artois as a reinforcement – the squadron received 11 pilots altogether, drawn from four Hurricane units.

Although having no combat experience, 'Hack' Russell was a skilled pilot, and just 24 hours after arriving in France he claimed four or five enemy aircraft destroyed – a mix of Bf 109Es and Henschel Hs 123 biplane ground attack aircraft, encountered near Louvain. With relevant squadron records pertaining to this mission long since lost, it has been difficult to ascertain whether Russell's claims were for aircraft destroyed, probably destroyed or just damaged.

The following afternoon (15 May) he enjoyed further success when he shared in the destruction of two He 111Hs of 9./KG 51 with Plt Off Peter Dixon. Russell's Hurricane I (P2619/'AF-D') was hit by return fire during the engagement, however, and the Australian was slightly wounded. Crash-landing the fighter, he was taken to a hospital in Paris and subsequently evacuated back to England. Due to the

ABOVE: Head bowed, deep in thought, acting flight commander Flg Off I B N 'Hack' Russell prepares to start up Spitfire I L1058/'PR-J' for the last time at Northolt on the afternoon of 1 June 1940. Within an hour of this photo being taken he was dead, having fallen victim to a lone Bf 110 off Dunkirk. Russell's mount on this ill-fated sortie was one of the oldest Spitfires on strength with No 609 Sqn at the time of its demise, having been delivered to the unit, via No 27 MU, from Supermarine's Woolston factory on 6 September 1939. The aircraft's heavy usage since its arrival in the frontline is clearly visible in this shot, with the paint worn away around the canopy rail and wing root.

RIGHT: L1065/'PR-E' was amongst the batch of 16 Supermarine fighters sent north to No 609 Sqn when it transitioned from the biplane Hind to the monoplane Spitfire I in August-September 1939. Arriving at the unit's Yeadon base on the same day as 'Hack' Russell's L1058, this aircraft saw service with the 'West Riding' Squadron until it was passed on to Training Command on 5 November 1940. A true combat veteran, L1065 survived almost five years of abuse at the hands of tyro fighter pilots in a series of OTUs, prior to finally being scrapped in 1947. Adorned with a 40-inch Type A fuselage roundel and lacking a fin flash, L1065 was photographed whilst on a routine convoy patrol from Drem in early 1940. Note also the original, production standard, 'thin' aerial mast.

chaos created by the invasion, No 607 Sqn was not informed of this, and Flg Off I B N Russell's name was entered in the unit's record book as 'missing, presumed killed'!

Within days of returning to the UK, Russell turned up at No 609 Sqn following 'instructions given to him by the Air Ministry', according to Frank Ziegler. Just 48 hours earlier the Spitfire unit had arrived at RAF Northolt from Drem, and it was in the process of readying itself for combat when Russell returned. Having briefly seen action, he was pumped by all the pilots on the unit for his combat experiences, as they anticipated their first dice with the enemy.

On 30 May No 609 Sqn was ordered to fly its first operational mission within No 11 Group, 12 Spitfire Is being despatched from Northolt to perform a wing-strength patrol over the Dunkirk beaches. Leading 'Green' Section was Flg Off 'Hack' Russell. Flown in bad weather, the wing failed to encounter the *Luftwaffe*, and a pilot was killed when he became lost upon returning to England, ran out of fuel and spun in.

The following day, operating out of North Weald, ten Spitfires performed an afternoon 'top patrol' over the evacuation beaches, and this time the enemy was encountered. Two He 111s were engaged, and 'Hack' Russell was duly credited with having destroyed one of them, subject to confirmation. A second Heinkel was also downed by No 609 Sqn, although Flt Lt 'Presser' Persse-Joynt was lost during the course of the patrol.

The unit launched a second patrol from North Weald at 19.00, with the nine Spitfires sent aloft being led by 'Hack' Russell. As soon as they arrived over Dunkirk, the Australian spotted a formation of 15 He 111s and 20 Bf 109s being bracketed by naval anti-aircraft shells. Quickly climbing to the bombers' altitude of 15,000 ft, Russell despatched a Heinkel (and possibly a second bomber) and then spotted that his No 3, Sgt Geoffrey Bennett, was under attack from one of the escorting Bf 109s. Breaking away from the bombers, he chased down the *Emil* and fired from just 100 yards. The German fighter lost six feet off its port wing and dived straight into the sea.

Now out of ammunition, Russell nursed Bennett in his shot up Spitfire back towards English coast until the latter bailed out three miles from Hawkinge. He remained overhead until he saw Bennett floating in his 'Mae West', then radioed for a rescue launch to pick up the downed pilot – 'Red 3' was rescued by the minesweeper HMS *Playboy*. Having recovered from his wounds, Flt Sgt G C Bennett eventually fell victim to Bf 109s again over the Channel on the morning of 29 April 1941, although this time he was not rescued.

News of the awarding of a DFC to 'Hack' Russell was received at Northolt on 31 May, this being the first such decoration bestowed upon a No 609 Sqn pilot – it was publicly gazetted on 14 June. The citation that accompanied this award stated that he had downed 'ten and six possibles', although post-war research has revealed that this should have read 'ten, including six possibles'.

ABOVE: All hailing from Leeds, Bradford and other West Riding cities, these groundcrew were typical of the men who kept No 609 Sqn's 15 Spitfires serviceable throughout the early war years. Whilst the squadron's complement of pre-war auxiliary pilots slowly dwindled in number as the conflict progressed, over 40 'local' groundcrew remained with No 609 Sqn well into 1941. Lacking a bullet-proof windscreen and still fitted with a two-speed propeller, this unidentified Spitfire I was photographed chocked at Drem during the winter of 1939-40.

Although having lost three pilots killed and one wounded in just two days of operations, No 609 Sqn put up nine aircraft for yet another afternoon patrol on 1 June. Split up into three three-aircraft sections, No 609 Sqn became scattered off Dunkirk, and as related by Flg Off A R 'Paul' Edge at the start of this account, 'Hack' Russell's section was bounced by a lone Bf 110, and the Australian's Spitfire I (L1058/'PR-J') swiftly shot down. The body of Flg Off Ian Bedford Nesbit Russell DFC was never found.

LEFT: Still settling into their new base at RAF Northolt just four days after arriving in the south-east, groundcrewmen enjoy a cigarette break in front of the recently-dug revetments at the Middlesex fighter station on 24 May 1940. Both of the Spitfires visible in this photograph have their undersides painted in the factory-applied Night, White and Aluminium scheme, over which 50-inch Type A roundels have been applied. The fighters are armed, fuelled and plugged into a starter trolley accumulator in readiness for the order to scramble.

The Battle of Britain

One of the greatest aerial engagements of the 20th Century officially commenced on 10 July 1940, and continued unabated until 31 October 1940. As with most campaigns, these dates are arbitrary, for the *Luftwaffe* had started its attacks on coastal shipping convoys in the first days of July (18 fighters had been lost and 13 pilots killed between 1 and 10 July), and continued daylight raids on targets in southern England well into November. However, from an official RAF standpoint the battle lasted for 113 days, and in order to qualify for the Battle of Britain Clasp to the 1939-45 Star, Fighter Command aircrew had to have flown operationally on at least one of these days.

Eleven Americans qualified for the Clasp, although only one would survive the war to wear this much respected decoration.

Come 10 July, just one of the four 'Yanks' who had been serving with Fighter Command at the start of the war remained in the frontline – Flg Off Carl Raymond Davis. He had seen his unit (No 601 Sqn) lose 11 Hurricanes during the defeat in France, followed by two pilots killed in action whilst participating in Operation *Dynamo*. Since then, the 'County of London' squadron had been flying several sorties a day in an effort to protect convoys sailing through the dangerous waters of the English Channel. And with the unit based on the Sussex coast at Tangmere, No 601 Sqn was very much in the frontline of this opening phase of the battle.

Tom Moulson described the daily routine that Carl Davis found himself in during these early engagements in his history of No 601 Sqn, *The Flying Sword*, published in 1964;

'Each pilot flew two days with one day off, a lorry taking him to dispersal on the airfield before dawn and bringing him back after a day's flying and air fighting – unless he was on night readiness – for a pint in the mess and a badly needed night's rest.

ABOVE: This photograph was one in a sequence taken by renowned aviation photographer Charles E Brown during a visit he made to Tangmere in early July 1940. This view shows a section of No 601 Sqn Hurricanes being fuelled (the aircraft to the left also appears to be having its magazines reloaded) prior to undertaking a convoy protection patrol off the south coast. The unit seems to be relying on a towable bowser to supply its fuel rather than the ubiquitous Albion three-point truck. Note also the belts of 0.303-in ammunition draped over the flat-loader trolley marked '601', the solitary fire extinguisher just forward of the bowser and the fitter holding the radio access panel for the Hurricane parked to the right of the photo. Three pilots are visible in this view, although only two have been identified – the individual in the pre-war white overall standing behind said radio fitter is Flg Off 'Willie' Rhodes-Moorhouse, whilst the pilot in the 'Mae West' behind the ammunition trolley is newly-promoted squadron OC, Sqn Ldr The Hon J W M 'Max' Aitken. Rhodes-Moorhouse would be killed in action on the morning of 6 September 1940, shot down in the same engagement as American Carl Davis.

LEFT: Another of the photographs taken by Charles E Brown at Tangmere during his early July 1940 visit. In the centre of the photograph, an armourer carefully feeds belted 0.303-in ammunition into the starboard wing magazines, whilst to his left a second airman fills the fuel tank. The muzzles for the aircraft's four starboard guns can just be seen protruding from the exposed wing leading edge. At the height of the Battle of Britain, experienced groundcrews could rearm and refuel a Hurricane or a Spitfire in as little as four minutes.

'The Hurricanes were parked nose-into-wind, their engines run up periodically to keep them warm between sorties. There were four stages of preparedness: "Released – off duty; "Available – fifteen minutes to get airborne; "Readiness" – five minutes; "Standby" – two minutes, which meant sitting strapped in the aircraft. The different categories of preparedness in themselves introduced an element of strain, an invisible tether of varying radius broken only by the end of day or the febrile bustle of a "scramble". Available was the bugbear of them all; there was no time to remove the cumbersome flying clothes or go very far, although one would probably spend hours inactively, and one of the fighter pilot's greatest anxieties was the possibility of being scrambled whilst on the lavatory.'

Having failed to open his account against the *Luftwaffe* during the fighting in France, Carl Davis claimed his first victory within 48 hours of the Battle of Britain officially starting. No 601 Sqn was kept very busy on 11 July, for it had downed a photo-recce Do 17P of 2.(F)/11 off the Isle of Wight at 10.14 hrs, followed by two Ju 87s and two Bf 110s near Portland naval base just over an hour later. The unit had arrived too late to prevent the bombing of the base, its Hurricanes being refuelled at Tangmere when the raid was detected by the Ventnor RDF site.

Determined not to be caught with fighters on the ground again, No 11 Group scrambled both flights of No 601 Sqn at 17.15 hrs when a smaller raid was detected heading for Portsmouth naval base. Amongst the men sent aloft was Carl Davis (in Hurricane I P3363), and his section successfully engaged the Bf 110C escorts whilst the rest of the squadron struck at the He 111Hs of I./KG 55. The American singled out a *Zerstörer* and swiftly shot it down near Lymington with a series of well-aimed bursts. Two Heinkels were also destroyed.

In return, the unit had Sgt Arthur Woolley shot down in flames by defensive anti-aircraft fire thrown up by batteries surrounding the naval base at Portsmouth. The pilot succeeded in bailing out with burns to his hands, and he subsequently returned to No 601 Sqn the following month – Woolley would be forced to take to his parachute twice more before the end of the battle!

No 601 Sqn was still making good losses in both men and machinery at this time, and on 12 July a second American arrived on the unit in the form of Plt Off William Meade Lindsley Fiske III, known universally as 'Billy'. A colourful character, his background is described in the following quote from *Over-Paid, Over-Sexed and Over-Here*, written in 1991 by Lt Col James A Goodson and Norman Franks;

'Although an American (born in Chicago in 1911), he was the son of an international New York millionaire stockbroker living in Paris. Despite his American citizenship, Billy Fiske was very much an Anglophile, for he had been educated at Trinity College, Cambridge, and later joined the London office of his father's company. In his spare time he had become a well known racing car driver and bob-sleigh champion, a first-rate shot, played golf and sailed a yacht. In fact he held a record for the Cresta Run at St Moritz and captained the US Olympic team that won the bob-sleigh event in 1932. He also drove in the 24-hour Le Mans race in a Stutz at just 19.

'Billy married Rose, the former Countess of Warwick, in 1939. He was the Golden Boy – good looks, wealth, charm, intelligence, he had it all. He excelled in most sports and was good in business. He was very American, but completely international at the same time. The English loved him, and he loved them.

'It was not surprising that someone like Billy should also want to fly, and in September 1939 he joined the RAF. In August he had been at the New York office, but returned to England on the *Aquitania* on the 30th. With his background it was natural that he "got fighters", and that he managed to get himself posted to 601 (Auxiliary) Squadron.'

According to Moulson's history of No 601 Sqn, the CO, Sqn Ldr Max Aitken, and his flight commanders 'admitted to some misgivings about this untried American adventurer, although Billy Fiske arrived at Tangmere with no pretensions or illusions'. One of those flight commanders was Flt Lt Sir Archibald Hope, who had led 'A' Flight since war was declared. His view on Fiske is most revealing:

'Unquestionably Billy Fiske was the best pilot I've ever known. It was unbelievable how good he was. He picked it up so fast, it wasn't true. He'd flown a bit before, but he was a natural as a fighter pilot. He was also terribly nice and extraordinarily modest. He fitted in to the squadron very well.'

Sadly, 'Billy' Fiske would survive in the frontline for just a matter of weeks.

Canadian Connection

When the Battle of Britain commenced in early July 1940, the USA was still almost 18 months away from entering the Second World War. And although its president, Franklin D Roosevelt, had great sympathy for the plight of Britain, he lead a government which stuck firmly to the isolationist policies that had characterised America's view of the world since the end of the Great War.

In order to ensure that the United States would not get involved in any future European conflict, Congress had passed a strict neutrality act in 1935. This covered numerous provisions, including the fact that Americans travelling on ships belonging to belligerent nations did so at their own risk. The act was further revised in 1936 and 1937, and clauses inserted that forbade US citizens from travelling on belligerent ships, or in a war zone. The Fourth Neutrality Act, which was passed in November 1939 by Congress in response to the German invasion of Poland and the declaration of war by Britain and France, only served to confirm the American government's firm stand on this issue.

Two months prior to this act being passed, a presidential proclamation had been made that specifically banned the recruiting of men for the armed forces of foreign countries from within the USA, and its territories. This ruling also made it illegal to 'hire someone to go beyond the territorial limits of the United Sates – to Canada, for example – to enlist in a foreign country's military'. The proclamation also stated that it was unlawful to use a US passport to secure passage to a foreign country for the purposes of enlistment, to travel anywhere on a belligerent ship or to embark on any vessel crossing the North Atlantic.

Despite these laws, a handful of American citizens could not resist the call to arms to fight for democracy against the tyranny of Nazism. For most, the easiest route to the war in Europe was via Canada. One individual who made the journey 'north of the border' before most was Otto John Peterson of Eckville, Atlanta. He joined the Royal Canadian Air Force (RCAF) on 7 November 1938 when aged 23 – details of his pre-service career remain undocumented.

Peterson was assigned to the newly-formed No 1 Sqn RCAF in the autumn of 1939, the unit receiving a handful of precious Hurricane Is from the batch of 20 supplied to Canada in 1938-39. The squadron had been mobilised at St Hubert, in Quebec, on 10 September 1939, and on 3 November its full complement of seven Hurricanes was sent to Dartmouth, Nova Scotia. Otto Peterson, and the rest of No 1 Sqn RCAF, remained at this base performing convoy patrols and other routine training flights until ordered overseas on 22 May 1940. The men boarded the steamship *Duchess of Atholl* in Halifax harbour on 8 June and set sail for Liverpool. Its Hurricanes were also shipped across to Britain, these aircraft making their second crossing of the Atlantic in little more than a year!

The unit was initially sent to RAF Middle Wallop, in Hampshire, on 21 June, where it was greeted by Air Chief Marshal Dowding. He enquired as to the state of the pilots' training, and

LEFT: Gloster-built Hurricane I R4218 served with No 601 Sqn from 15 August until 7 October, when it was written off in a forced landing following combat over Portland. During this period the fighter was used predominantly by Australian-born ace Howard Mayers, who claimed two Do 17s and a Bf 110 destroyed, two Do 17s damaged and a half-share in a probable Bf 110 all whilst flying R4218. Indeed, it was Mayers who was at the controls of Hurricane when it was hit in the glycol tank by enemy fire whilst engaging raiders sent to bomb the Westland aircraft factory at Yeovil on the afternoon of 7 October.

arranged for examples of the latest production-standard Hurricanes (with a three-bladed variable-pitch propeller, metal wings, additional protective armour and a Barr & Stroud GM 2 reflector gunsight) to be issued to the unit to supplement its early-build fighters. The first practice flight by No 1 Sqn RCAF was performed on 26 June, and Plt Off Peterson also took to British skies for the first time soon after this date.

On 4 July the unit moved to Croydon Airport, which had become a semi-permanent base within No 11 Group upon the declaration of war. Over the next few weeks No 1 Sqn RCAF flew a number of practice bomber interceptions with friendly Blenheims, whilst its CO, Sqn Ldr Ernie McNab was temporarily attached to the co-located No 111 Sqn to gain combat experience. For Otto Peterson, his first operational mission was just a matter of days away.

Tally-Ho! Yankee in a Spitfire

Arriving in the UK at around the same time as Otto Peterson was Arthur Gerald 'Art' Donahue, who had also followed the Canadian route to Fighter Command. The son of Mid-West farmers, born and raised in St Charles, Minnesota, Donahue had learned to fly at just 18. Barnstorming, pleasure flying, instructing and working as an aircraft mechanic throughout the 1930s, he ended up as an instructor at the grandly-named International Flying School in Laredo, Texas, in 1938.

Author of *Tally-Ho! Yankee in a Spitfire*, published in 1941, Donahue hardly viewed himself as fighter pilot material at this time:

'As I remember, when I started flying there were about 120 licensed pilots in Minnesota, and if you had lined us all up at that time and ranked us according to our possibilities of ever flying in a war, I'd have been in about 119th place. I didn't have any of the qualifications of a soldier. I was neither big nor very strong. I was quite mild-tempered and absolutely afraid to fight, and I was more cautious in my flying than the average pilot then.'

When war broke out in Europe, 'Art' Donahue felt the need 'to volunteer at once for England'. However, in consideration for his family, he instead applied for a commission in the US Army Air Corps Reserve. After months of awaiting a reply to his request, he instead chose to head north for Canada when he heard that the RAF was hiring American pilots for 'non-combatant jobs'. He signed up in late June, and on 7 July he 'arrived in an English port on a dreary, foggy Sunday morning after a final 24 hours of constant zigzagging by our ship to upset the aim of any lurking enemy submarines'.

Just six days after first setting foot in Britain, the now Plt Off A G Donahue arrived at RAF Hawarden, south of Liverpool, to learn to fly Spitfires with No 7 Operational Training Unit (OTU). His fellow course mates were a mix of British, Polish and Belgian pilots. After a few days of flying in a Harvard I advanced trainer, Donahue was introduced to the Spitfire:

'To myself, who had been instructing for the last year and a half in trainers of 40 horsepower that cruised at 60 miles per hour, this was such a change that there didn't seem to be any connection with my former flying. The first time I took a Spitfire up, I felt more like a passenger than a pilot.'

"I felt drawn into the struggle like a moth to a candle…"

'ART' DONAHUE

Typical of the American volunteer pilots to see action prior to the arrival of the US Army Air Forces in late 1942, 'Art' Donahue expressed his reasons for putting his life on the line for Britain during the summer of 1940 in the following extract from *Tally-Ho! Yankee in a Spitfire*:

'It's hard to give a specific reason why I became a combat pilot. Of course I'd always wanted to be one; and once I was in England the significance of the struggle seemed to carry me away. This was mid-July. France had fallen, and the invasion of England seemed imminent. Its success would open the whole world to a barbarian conquest. I had a growing admiration for the British people and a sincere desire to help them all I could. I couldn't help feeling that it would be fighting for my country, too.

'I felt drawn into the struggle like a moth to a candle. That's a pretty good comparison, too, for it developed that I was to get burned once and be drawn right back into it again!

'Knowing that one of England's greatest problems was inferiority in numbers in the air, I felt it a duty as a follower of the civilised way of life to throw my lot in if they would take me. To fight side by side with these people against the enemies of civilisation would be the greatest of all privileges. I had never done any military flying, but was confident of my ability to adapt myself.

'Inquiries revealed that the way was wide open. I could be a fighter (pursuit) pilot if I wished, by first taking an advanced training course. Also I could probably get where the fighting was heaviest if I wished because pilots as a rule were given preference in this regard. I was given a commission as a pilot officer and was allowed two days' leave to buy a uniform. I was impressed with the swiftness and lack of red tape with which I was accepted. I had simply shown them that I had the goods and they had said in effect: "All right. We'll buy. Sign here, and you can start delivering". It was a refreshing contrast to my experiences in my own country.'

Being an experienced aviator, Donahue soon got to grips with his new mount, and by the end of July he was deemed ready to enter the fray. His wish to serve in the frontline came true in spades, for he was posted on 3 August to No 64 Sqn at RAF Kenley, right in the heart of No 11 Group – fellow No 7 OTU graduate Plt Off Peter Kennard-Davis (aged just 19) accompanied Donahue to the unit. This outfit had had seven pilots killed in action, one captured and one wounded since first encountering the *Luftwaffe* during Operation *Dynamo*.

No 64 Sqn's most recent losses had been suffered on the afternoon of 25 July over the Channel, when Flg Off Alistair Jeffrey and Sub-Lt Francis Paul were downed protecting a westbound coastal convoy off Dover from attack by an overwhelming force of fighters and bombers. Both men were experienced pre-war military pilots with victories to their credit (Jeffrey was subsequently awarded a posthumous DFC). In contrast, Donahue and Kennard-Davis were novices in the deadly art of aerial combat, and this fact would soon be cruelly exposed.

'Andy', 'Red' and 'Shorty'

'Art' Donahue was not the only American at Hawarden in July 1940, for on the course directly after him were no less than three 'Yanks' – Eugene Quimby 'Red' Tobin, Vernon Charles 'Shorty' Keough and Andrew 'Andy' Mamedoff. Unlike Donahue, this trio were motivated, initially at least, more by money and a sense of adventure than by the thought of saving the free world!

All three men had been recruited in America by an agent working on behalf of Col Charles Sweeny, co-founder of the 'Eagle Squadrons' (see Chapter Four for details). Tobin and Mamedoff, who both held private pilots licences, had initially signed up to fight for the Finns in the Russo-Finnish Winter War. Tempted by the offer of an all-expenses paid trip to Helsinki, and $100 a month once in the frontline, the two were on the verge of setting off for Scandinavia when the war came to an abrupt end. Not wishing to lose face with family and friends, they agreed to head for France instead, Tobin being quoted as saying at the time, 'If you going looking for a fight, you can always find one'.

Tobin and Mamedoff boarded a freighter in Nova Scotia, having met up with the diminutive (4 ft 10.5 in) figure of 'Shorty' Keough along the way. Brooklyn-born Keough had earned a living as a professional parachutist at fairs and carnivals along the American East Coast, his colourful past rivalling that of Tobin, who had grown up in Hollywood and worked as an MGM studio messenger, and Mamedoff, who was the son of 'White' Russian émigrés!

ABOVE: Veteran No 601 Sqn Hurricane I P3886 is seen being serviced on the eastern fringe of the perimeter at Exeter Airport in mid-September 1940. Note the aircraft's natural metal cowling over its reduction gear, which had been fitted in the wake of the engine failure suffered by the Hurricane on 26 July. Once repaired, the fighter enjoyed success whilst being flown by No 601 Sqn aces Sgt Len Guy (who shared in the destruction of a Ju 88 on 15 August) and Flg Off Carl Davis (one Ju 87 destroyed and a second shared destroyed, as well as a Bf 109E destroyed on 18 August, followed by a Bf 110 probable 13 days later). Both pilots had been killed in action by the time this photograph was taken, Guy being shot down over Portsmouth on 18 August and Davis crashing to his death near Tunbridge Wells on 6 September.

Hawker Hurricane I P3886 of No 601 'County of London' Sqn, Tangmere, August 1940
Flg Off Carl Davis scored two and one shared kills in this Hurricane on 18 August 1940. P3886 later served with No 1 Sqn, before enduring a spell in Training Command (with No 59 OTU) and subsequent conversion into a Merchant Ship Fighter Unit aircraft. Duly passed on to No 253 Sqn in North Africa, P3886 ended its days in India in 1944.

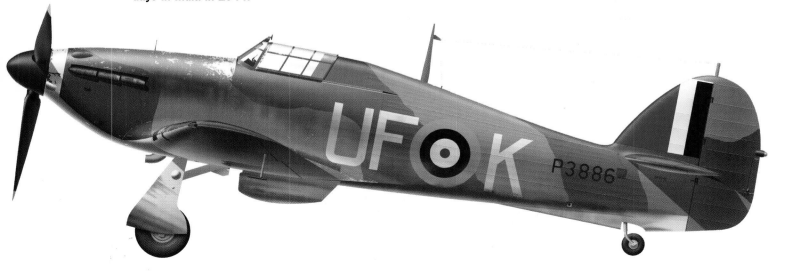

LEFT: Aside from the two Ju 87s credited to Carl Davis in Hurricane P3886 on 18 August, he had forced this Stuka down two days earlier after chasing it across the Sussex coast at low level in P3383. Riddled with the best part of 240 rounds of 0.303-in ammunition, the aircraft crash-landed at Bowley Farm, near South Mundham, during the devastating raid on Tangmere on the afternoon of the 16th. Its crew, Oberfeldwebel Witt and Feldwebel Röcktäschel of 3./StG 2, both died of wounds received during the engagement, with the Feldwebel gunner killed prior to the Ju 87 hitting the ground. Witt died of his injuries soon after the dive-bomber came to a halt, its port outer wing section ripped off by a tree and its propeller shattered through striking the ground. Remarkably, the Stuka's undercarriage remained intact in spite of the aircraft's heavy impact with several trees and a hedgerow.

By the time the three American 'mercenaries' arrived in France, the *Blitzkrieg* had erupted, and they spent the next few weeks retreating steadily south from Paris towards Bordeaux, just one step ahead of the German army. Tobin again had a suitable quote to describe their time in France: 'Aw hell, we had a million laffs'.

Succeeding in getting the last ship to depart St Jean-de-Luz bound for England, they applied to join the RAF upon arriving in Britain. However, the Air Ministry had full respect for America's strict neutrality laws, and advised the trio to return to Canada and try applying from there after having first joined the RCAF. Not to be detered, the trio successfully pleaded their case to a Member of Parliament, whose name they had been given through their initial contact with Col Sweeny. Tobin, Keough and Mamedoff were duly accepted into the RAF on 5 July 1940 as pilot officers, and within days they had arrived at Hawarden.

After four weeks of training all three men were posted to No 609 Sqn at RAF Middle Wallop (or 'RAF Centre Punch' as Tobin soon dubbed it), arriving at the Hampshire airfield in No 10 Group on 6 August. The Americans were replacements for three pre-war auxiliary pilots who had been deemed to be either too old (Flt Lt Stephen Beaumont, aged 30) or medically unfit for frontline flying (Flg Off Bernard Little and Plt Off Jarvis Blayney). A seasoned flight commander from co-located No 238 Sqn was also posted in at this time, along with two Poles from Hawarden.

No 609 Sqn's Plt Off David Crook described his new American squadronmates in telling detail in his autobiography *Spitfire Pilot*, published in 1942:

'They were typical Americans, amusing, always ready with some devastating wisecrack (frequently at the expense of authority), and altogether excellent company. Our three Yanks became quite an outstanding feature of the squadron.

'Andy was dark, tough, and certainly rather good-looking with his black hair and flashing eyes.

'Red was very tall and lanky, and possessed the most casual manner and general outlook on life that I ever saw. I don't believe he ever batted an eyelid about anything, except possibly the increasing difficulty of getting his favourite "rye high". After a fight he never showed the slightest trace of excitement, and I remember that after one afternoon's fairly concentrated bombing of the aerodrome, during which a number of people were killed, he turned up grinning as usual, but with his clothes in an awful mess and covered in white chalk because he had to throw himself several times into a chalk pit as the Huns dropped out of the clouds. He made only the grinning comment, 'Aw hell, I had a million laffs'.

ABOVE:
The Ju 87 downed by Carl Davis has the unused 7.92 mm ammunition stripped from its wing guns by armourers from nearby Tangmere. Note the heavy impact damage to the Stuka's wing root and outer section.

'Shorty was the smallest man I ever saw, barring circus freaks, but he possessed a very stout size in hearts. When he arrived in the squadron we couldn't believe that he would ever reach the rudder bar in a Spit; apparently the Medical Board thought the same and refused to have him at first, as he was much shorter than the RAF minimum requirements. However, Shorty insisted on having a trial, and he produced two cushions which he had brought all the way from the States via France, especially for this purpose. One went under his parachute and raised him up, the other he wedged in the small of his back, and thus he managed to fly a Spitfire satisfactorily, though in the machine all you could see of him was the top of his head and a couple of eyes peering over the edge of the cockpit.'

All three men were keen to get at the *Luftwaffe*, but their CO, Sqn Ldr Horace Darley, was fully aware of their inexperience. He therefore ordered that they undertake a further period of training within the unit prior being thrown into operational flying. After travelling thousands of miles to see combat, and having been chased out of France by the Germans without being given the opportunity to fight, 'Andy', 'Red' and 'Shorty' were now just days away from engaging the *Luftwaffe*.

Channel Clash

On the very day that Plt Offs Tobin, Keough and Mamedoff arrived at No 609 Sqn, Plt Off 'Art' Donahue got his first taste of combat. Unlike his countrymen posted to No 10 Group, Donahue would not be gradually eased into action for No 64 Sqn was short of pilots, and the German offensive against No 11 Group was increasing in intensity with the passing of every day. He performed a solitary familiarisation patrol on the afternoon of the 4th, and then set off from Kenley with five other Spitfires for the unit's forward base at Hawkinge the following morning.

En route to the Channel coast, No 64 Sqn was ordered to climb to 20,000 ft to relieve No 615 Sqn, which had been patrolling between Beachy Head and Dover. A convoy was headed

ABOVE: For many years William Meade Lindsley 'Billy' Fiske was officially deemed to have been the only American killed during the Battle of Britain, but recent research has revealed that he was actually the first of four US citizens to die during the campaign whilst serving with Fighter Command. A wealthy stockbroker, film producer and international sportsman, as well as the husband of the ex-Countess of Warwick, Fiske joined No 601 Sqn in July 1940, having never even flown a Hurricane! Effectively trained 'on the job', he proved a gifted fighter pilot, and saw near-daily action from 20 July through to his death on 17 August from wounds received in combat on the previous day.

through the narrow straits off the Kent coast, and a *Luftwaffe* attack was expected at any time. The two Spitfire sections were being led by No 64 Sqn's OC, Sqn Ldr A R D 'Don' MacDonnell, who would remain in charge of the unit throughout the Battle of Britain, and claim ten kills by the end of November.

As the fighter controller's calls became more specific, and his warning of bandits in the area heightened the tension, Donahue began to realise the enormity of the situation he now found himself in:

'My pulses pounded, and my thoughts raced. This was *it!*

'Our leader now led us upward in a steeper climb than I had ever dreamed an airplane could perform. Trembling with excitement, trying to realise that this was actually happening and I wasn't dreaming, I pulled the guard of my firing button. For the first time in my life I was preparing to kill! The button was painted red, and it looked strangely grim now that it was uncovered. I turned its safety ring, which surrounded it, from the position which read "SAFE" to the position which read "FIRE".'

No 64 Sqn was now patrolling in tight battle formation just off the Calais coast. Donahue then spotted a lone fighter some distance away from the formation, and just as he was about to inform MacDonnell, the CO transmitted the RAF 'battle cry' '*Tally-ho!*', and the unit dived on a gaggle of aircraft some distance away from the 'dot' that the American had spied. Having been told by MacDonnell that pilots could pick their own targets after the 'Tally-ho' had been given, Donahue did just that and dived away from his squadronmates after the solitary German aircraft, which turned out to be a Bf 109E of I./JG 54.

The American's combat inexperience was quickly revealed, for he missed with his first burst and then lost his quarry as it took violent evasive action. Spotting it once again, and manoeuvring back onto its tail, Donahue was just about to fire a second burst at the fleeing *Emil* when his own aircraft (Spitfire I K9991) was struck:

'*Powp!*'

'It sounded exactly as if some one had blown up a big paper bag and burst it behind my ears; and it shook the plane and was followed by a noise like hail on a tin roof.

'I realised that I had been hit somewhere behind me in my machine by a second Hun, and guessed that it was an exploding cannon shell that made the noise.'

Donahue now had two *Emils* to contend with, and in one of the rare examples of aircraft dogfighting during the Battle of Britain, he proceeded to fight for the advantage over the French coast for the next ten minutes. Although a combat novice, the American was a veteran pilot, having almost 2000 flying hours to his credit. Using all his skill, he succeeded in getting his battle-damaged Spitfire onto the tail of one of his assailants, and just as he was about to open fire he noticed that he gunsight was not working. In the seconds it took to try and find the fault, he was a sitting duck for the second *Emil*, which latched onto Donahue's tail once again.

Getting increasingly hot, tired and sweaty, and with little chance of defending himself, Donahue relied simply on instinctive flying to stay alive:

'During those next few minutes I think I must have blacked out at least 20 times in turns. I remember starting to spin at least once from turning too violently. I wanted to flee but couldn't get my directions straight because I was manoeuvring so fast. My compass couldn't help me unless I'd give it the chance to settle down. It was spinning like a top.'

Eventually, he extricated himself from the fight and made a break for the Dover coast. His enemies briefly followed him, but after he started to turn back into them as if to re-commence the dogfight, they broke off and headed for France. Once safely down at Hawkinge, Donahue's damaged Spitfire was examined by pilots and groundcrew alike. A cannon shell had exploded in the fuselage just behind the cockpit, severing the cabling that actuated the rudder trim and badly damaging the main elevator and rudder cables – it had also shorted the power supply for the gunsight. K9991 would not fly again with No 64 Sqn, and 'Art' Donahue 'hitched' a lift back to Kenley in the squadron's two-seat Magister 'hack' aircraft.

Claims for seven Bf 109s destroyed were made by the unit following this engagement (wartime *Luftwaffe* documentation reveals that just two fighters were lost), and in return Sgt Lewis Isaac was posted missing in action. He had been the 'weaver' protecting the rear of the

No 64 Sqn formation, and had been bounced by enemy fighters that had not been seen by the rest of his unit.

'Art' Donahue had survived his first action, and after two days of routine flying, on 8 August he participated in the now legendary Battle of Convoy CW 9, codenamed *PEEWIT*. The numerous actions fought on this day were for many years selected by historians as denoting the start of the Battle of Britain proper. The *Luftwaffe's Luftflotte* 3 was fully committed on the 8th, and its fighters, bombers and dive-bombers succeeded in shattering the 29-ship convoy, but at a heavy cost to themselves. All along the south coast Fighter Command Spitfires and Hurricanes duelled with Bf 109Es, Bf 110Cs, Ju 87Bs and Ju 88As.

No 64 Sqn scrambled all 12 of its Spitfires in the late morning from Hawkinge, although it failed to engage the enemy for almost an hour – by which time half the force had returned to base to refuel. The six fighters were then bounced by an estimated 30 *Emils* from II and III./JG 26, which had been instructed to sweep the Straits of Dover clear of RAF fighters ahead of a massive raid by 57 Ju 87s of *Luftlotte* 3 on the *PEEWIT* convoy.

The Spitfires scattered and went after individual targets, 'Art' Donahue succeeding in hitting one Bf 109 with at least four bursts, although he failed to claim this as having even been damaged upon his return to base. Two *Emils* were claimed as destroyed by the squadron, with Sqn Ldr MacDonnell and Sgt Jack Mann sharing in the destruction of *Oblt.* Willi Oehm's Bf 109E-4 – the former instructor was killed on his first operational flight with III./JG 26, his fighter crashing into the Channel.

LEFT: Ironically, of the handful of photographs to feature No 64 Sqn Spitfire Is during the Battle of Britain, most were taken by the Luftwaffe! One in a series of shots exposed in a beet field on the French coast near the airfield at Calais-Marck on the afternoon of 15 August, this view shows a battle-damaged K9964 soon after the fighter had force-landed. Its pilot, Plt Off Ralph Roberts, reported to his captors that he had become lost after a particularly vicious dogfight over the Channel. Straying over occupied France, the Spitfire had been 'bounced' by Bf 109Es of the 7th Staffel Schwarm of JG 26 and shot down by Leutnant Gerhard Müller-Duhe – who would in turn lose his life when shot down by Flt Lt 'Pete' Brothers over Chilham just three days later.

No 64 Sqn had not escaped unscathed, however, for 'Art' Donahue's buddy, Plt Off Peter Kennard-Davis, had bailed out of his Spitfire I (L1039) with serious wounds. He survived in the Royal Victoria Hospital for two days, but succumbed to his injuries on 10 August.

'Art' Donahue had little time to grieve for his young friend from No 7 OTU, for he was involved in two action-packed patrols with the unit on the 11th, and then on the afternoon of the 12th was himself shot down. Having completed an uneventful sortie in the early afternoon, No 64 Sqn was scrambled to intercept bombers heading for No 11 Group's airfields and radar stations. The squadron was vectored in the direction of 18 Do 17s of KG 2 that had attacked RAF Manston, but prior to intercepting the bombers, the unit ran straight into their escorts, which Donahue erroneously identified as 20 'white Heinkel He 113s' – these aircraft were actually Bf 109Es of I./JG 26.

Having got separated from his section during the opening seconds of the engagement, Donahue found himself alone chasing a solitary 'He 113'. He positioned himself behind the

Supermarine Spitfire I K9964 of No 64 Sqn, Kenley, August 1940

This ex-No 602 Sqn Spitfire I was on strength with No 64 Sqn when Plt Off 'Art' Donahue arrived fresh from No 7 OTU on 3 August 1940. Twelve days later the fighter was forced down in a beet field on the French coast near the Luftwaffe airfield at Calais-Marck. Note how the fighter's serial was painted out with a solid rectangle of dark earth paint.

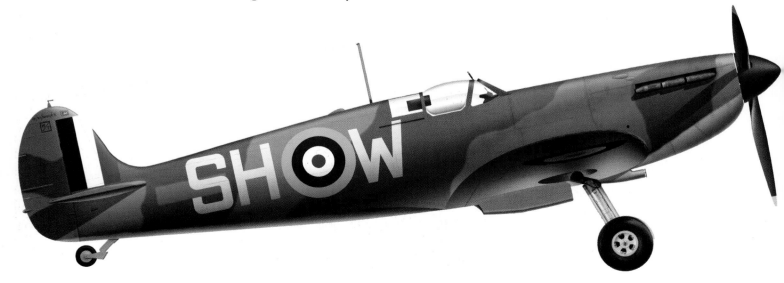

RIGHT: Newly-commissioned Plt Off A G 'Art' Donahue poses for a formal photograph soon after collecting his uniform in London in early July. Fresh-faced, and keen to tackle the Germans, he would be shot down and seriously wounded within nine days of arriving on No 64 Sqn at Kenley.

unsuspecting fighter as it skimmed along the tops of a bank of cloud, and just as he was about to fire, his Spitfire I (X4018) was struck a series of mortal blows by the *Emil* of either *Fw.* Gerhard Gryzmalla or *Lt.* Heinz Ebeling of 8./JG 26. Both men were skilled combat pilots, with Ebeling having already claimed two Hurricanes (from either Nos 151 or 501 Sqns) destroyed during an earlier sortie that same day – he was made PoW in early November, having claimed 18 kills.

'Art' Donahue was in serious trouble, for his elevator and rudder cables were completely severed, although his aileron controls still functioned. As he desperately tried to roll into the cloud bank below him, the American was hit again:

'The din and confusion were awful inside the cockpit. I remember seeing some of the instrument panel breaking up, and holes dotting the gas tank in front of me. Smoke trails of tracer bullets appeared right inside the cockpit. Bullets were going between my legs, and I remember seeing a bright flash of an incendiary bullet going past my leg and into the gas tank.'

Within seconds his Spitfire was on fire, and having already pulled his canopy back, Donahue released the locking pin that secured his seat straps and started to climb out. Just as he was in the process of extricating himself, the cockpit was engulfed in flames, and the pilot received serious burns to his hands, wrists, forearms and face. Dragged out of his aircraft by the 200-mph slipstream, the wounded Donahue deployed his parachute and floated gently down to earth

BELOW: Of the 11 Americans to see action with Fighter Command during the Battle of Britain, three of them served side-by-side with No 609 'West Riding' Sqn at Middle Wallop in August-September 1940. Plt Offs 'Andy' Mamedoff (left), 'Shorty' Keough (centre) and 'Red' Tobin (right) pose for one of a series of photographs in, on and around a borrowed Hurricane known to have been decorated with a Polish air force marking below the exhaust stubs. This official Air Ministry shot was taken in October 1940 following the formation of No 71 'Eagle' Sqn at RAF Church Fenton.

RIGHT: Spitfire I 'PR-Q' (serial unknown) has its guns fired into the butts at Drem, in Scotland, during early April 1940. Although not strictly a Battle of Britain photograph, this aircraft did go on to see action with the unit during the summer, flying from Middle Wallop. Note the photographers crouched forward of the aircraft's port wing. Such firepower demonstrations proved popular with the press, although they formed no part of the standard checking procedure for the Spitfire's armament.

near Sellindge, east of Ashford in Kent. He would spend the next four weeks in a hospital in Canterbury undergoing treatment for burns to his hands and arms, and recovering from shrapnel wounds to his right leg.

By the time 'Art' Donahue returned to No 64 Sqn, the battle-weary unit had been moved north to Leconfield, in No 13 Group, in order to rest and re-equip.

'Flying Swordsmen'

After a hectic July, No 601 Sqn was to enjoy no respite come August. In fact, its operational tempo increased markedly as the month wore on, the enemy switching its tactics from bombing

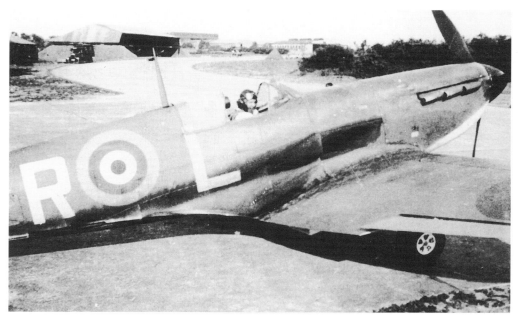

BELOW LEFT: Photographed on the eve of the battle, Spitfire I P9322 'PR-L' is seen taxying out from its dispersal at Northolt on 1 July. Strapped into the cockpit is Plt Off David Crook, who would claim a Ju 87 destroyed and a second Stuka damaged whilst flying the fighter on 9 July. P9322 was in turn badly holed by cannon rounds fired from a Bf 110C of V.(Z)/LG 1 on 8 August, its pilot on this occasion, Plt Off Michael Appleby, having already downed a Zerstörer just minutes prior to his fighter being hit. Spitfire I R6699 was duly re-coded 'PR-L', and on 18 August it struck a parked No 604 Sqn Blenheim IF at Middle Wallop soon after 'Red' Tobin had landed at the end of a patrol. Although suffering damage to its flaps and tail, R6699 was quickly returned to full serviceability.

convoys and naval bases to striking directly at fighter airfields in Nos 10 and 11 Groups, as well as the all-important radar stations along the south coast. Due to its location on the West Sussex coast, Tangmere could send its fighters to protect targets in both groups, and No 601 Sqn had being doing just that since early July.

Flg Off Carl Davis and fellow American Plt Officer 'Billy' Fiske had been involved in most of the interceptions flown by the unit in the weeks since the latter pilot had arrived at Tangmere. Although both 29 years old, and from well-to-do families, in terms of actual flying experience the two men were poles apart. Davis had served with No 601 Sqn since 1936, and had more than 1,500 flying hours in his log book (400 on Hurricanes alone). Fiske had learned to fly in early 1940, and had arrived at the unit having never even sat in a Hurricane! Having clocked up 11 hours on the Hawker fighter at Tangmere, he flew his first operational sortie on 20 July, and never looked back from there.

By 16 August Carl Davis had downed four Bf 110s (including three on the previous day, which had been designated *Adlertag*, or 'Eagle Day', by the *Luftwaffe* to denote the start of its campaign against RAF airfields), claimed a further three *Zerstörer* as probables and damaged two more. He had also shared in the probable destruction of a Ju 88 and damaged a second Junkers bomber, as well as a single Bf 109. Fiske, too, had also proven his worth as a fighter pilot during this period, having damaged a Bf 110 whilst leading a section on 11 August, followed by a Ju 88 confirmed destroyed and a second probably destroyed 24 hours later. On the 13th he was credited with two Bf 110s probably destroyed and a further two damaged.

On 15 August a series of five huge raids were launched by the *Luftwaffe*, hitting airfields and industrial targets across southern England. No 601 Sqn was one of four squadrons which intercepted the late afternoon assault by 60 Ju 88As of LG 1 (escorted by 40 Bf 110s of ZG 2) on the airfields at Middle Wallop and Worthy Down, the unit enjoying particular success against the bombers that struck the latter site. Indeed, 4./LG 1 lost five out of seven Ju 88s sortied that day to the pilots of the 'County of London' squadron. One of those to enjoy success was Carl Davis, who claimed a Junkers bomber over Bishop Waltham at 17.45 hrs. This kill took his tally to exactly five, and made him the sole American ace of the Battle of Britain. According to the squadron diary, 'Billy' Fiske also succeeded in manoeuvring a straggling Ju 88 into the Portsmouth balloon barrage, having exhausted his ammunition.

No 601 Sqn had performed extraordinarily well in the face of daunting odds on the 15th, but its handful of pilots had little time to rest on their laurels. Tangmere had been attacked that day for the first time in the battle, and 24 hours later it would be severely bombed.

The 'County of London' squadron was scrambled at 12.25 hrs as a massive raid was detected heading for the south coast.

BELOW: Another view of 'PR-L' having its magazines restocked with 0.303-in ammunition. When an airman from No 609 Sqn saw a Spitfire taxy into dispersal with its gun covers missing and wing undersurfaces streaked with powder fouling, his standard question to the pilot was 'Bags of joy, Sir?'. Invariably, the reply would be an emphatic 'Yes!'

ABOVE: The second 'PR-L' is seen being hastily rearmed at Warmwell late in the afternoon of 13 August, having just returned from a successful sortie over Weymouth with Plt Off Crook at the controls. R6699 had been used by the future author of 'Spitfire Pilot' to destroy the Bf 109E-1 of 5./JG 53's Unteroffizier Willi Hohenfeldt, who was captured. Note the pilot's parachute slung over the tailplane and missing canvas gun port patches.

LEFT: Conspicuous by his lack of a 'Mae West', Plt Off 'Red' Tobin was reluctantly roped in for this group shot, which was taken at Warmwell soon after the unit had returned from its epic battle with the Luftwaffe on the afternoon of 13 August – now better known as 'Adlertag', or 'Eagle Day'. Thirteen aircraft had been scrambled to intercept Ju 87s of II./StG 2 that had been sent to attack Warmwell and Middle Wallop, the dive-bombers being escorted by Bf 109Es from I./JG 53. During a brief, but frenzied, attack, six Stukas and two Emils were destroyed witmhout loss (two Spitfires were damaged, however). Tobin did not participate in this mission, as he was still three days away from being declared operational.

Dodging freshly filled bomb craters, the unit climbed as one to 20,000 ft over Bembridge, where its controller ordered the pilots to orbit and await the arrival of the enemy. Leading the unit was acting squadron leader Flt Lt Sir Archibald Hope. He was repeatedly instructed by the controller not to attack the 'Big Boys' (bombers), as No 601 Sqn was to provide top cover for a second squadron that had been given the task of performing this job. However, when he spotted close to 50 Ju 87s of StG 2 diving on an unprotected Tangmere, he ordered his men headlong into the fray.

They arrived too late to save their station, which was struck a series of devastating blows that destroyed the two remaining Belfast hangars, workshops, stores, sick quarters and shelters. The Officers' Mess was also badly damaged, and six Blenheims, seven Hurricanes and a Magister were either totally wrecked or badly damaged. Ten RAF personnel and three civilians were also killed, and a further 20 wounded.

The *Luftwaffe* paid a heavy price for this success, with almost every No 601 Sqn pilot claiming either a Stuka or a Bf 109 destroyed, including Carl Davis, who downed a single Ju 87 at low level. Extracts from the American's Combat Report for this mission reveal that he was leading 'Yellow' section during the engagement, and that No 601 Sqn dived from 20,000 ft down to 2000 ft to effect an interception. The Stukas had dropped their bombs and were heading south for the Sussex coast by the time the Hurricanes caught up with them, Davis quickly singling one out and pressing home his attack:

'I closed with one Ju 87 and after several bursts he went down under control and landed between Pagham and Bognor, crashing through some trees in a hedge. No one got out. Heavy fire, fairly accurate, and violent evasive action were employed by the Ju 87. My aircraft was hit in the radiator so I returned to Tangmere and landed at 13.05 hrs. I fired 30 rounds per gun.'

'Billy' Fiske had also tangled with the main Ju 87 force over Bognor Regis, and whilst seeking out a target, his Hurricane (P3358) had been struck in the reserve tank immediately forward of the cockpit. This had exploded, causing his fighter to burn fiercely. Instructed by his controller to bail out, Fiske replied calmly: 'No, I think I can save the kite. I'm coming in'.

His decision appeared to be the right one, for the fire quickly burnt itself out and Fiske glided in over the airfield boundary with nothing more than a thin ribbon of smoke emanating from the engine to denote his predicament. The Hurricane touched down and rolled along the grass runway, and all seemed fine until its pilot failed to spot a fresh bomb crater in his path. The fighter crashed heavily into the hole and blew up.

Fuel and ammunition exhausted, 'Archie' Hope landed back at the shattered station just minutes later, and he rushed to Fiske's burning Hurricane:

ABOVE: This Spitfire I (N3024 'PR-H') was lost near Weymouth on 14 August whilst being flown by Flg Off Henry 'Mac' Goodwin. Scrambled in the wake of the devastating surprise raid on Middle Wallop by Ju 88s of 1./LG 1, Goodwin (who had claimed three kills in the previous two days) headed south and simply disappeared. Flying alone, he was almost certainly 'bounced' by enemy fighters, for a Spitfire was seen to crash into the sea off Boscombe Pier, in Dorset, a short while later. The pilot succeeded in bailing out, but no trace of him could be found. Ten days later 'Mac' Goodwin's body was washed ashore on the Isle of Wight. This photograph shows a mission-ready N3024, and its groundcrew, at Middle Wallop in early August. Parked behind 'PR-H' is Spitfire I L1096 'PR-G', which survived its long spell with No 609 Sqn, and was later passed on to the Fleet Air Arm.

LEFT: Aside from the three 'Yanks' that served with No 609 Sqn during the battle, the Canadians also had a presence in the 'West Riding' squadron in the form of Plt Off Keith Ogilvie. A future ace, the Ottawan arrived on the unit on 20 August, and served in the frontline until shot down and captured on 4 July 1941. He subsequently took part in the Great Escape in March 1944, but was recaptured after two days on the run. Ogilvie is seen here smoking his pipe and enjoying a joke with 'Red' Tobin whilst at readiness in front of No 609 Sqn's Watch Office at Middle Wallop – both pilots were assigned to 'A' Flight, and regularly flew together. Note the American's preference for flying boots (into which he has tucked a map) and full service dress.

'As I came down, I saw one of our aircraft on its belly, belching smoke. It must have got a bullet in its engine.

'I taxied up to it and got out. There were two ambulancemen there. They had got Billy Fiske out of the cockpit. He was lying on the ground there. The ambulancemen didn't know how to take his parachute off, so I showed them. Billy was burnt about the hands and ankles, so I told them to put on Tanafax, the stuff we were supposed to put on burns. I'm told now its one of the worst things you could put on a burn. I told Billy: "Don't worry. You'll be alright", got back into my aeroplane and taxied back to the squadron. Our adjutant went to see him in hospital that night. Billy was sitting up in bed, perky as hell. The next we heard, he was dead. Died of shock.'

ABOVE: A panoramic view of No 609 Sqn's dispersal at the southern end of Middle Wallop during the height of the Battle of Britain. The Watch Office seen behind Plt Offs Ogilivie and Tobin in the photograph on the previous page is to the left of the large tent. The main Andover-Salisbury road (the A343) ran immediately behind this cluster of buildings, and Spitfires would regularly taxy along the public highway when being moved to and from the permanent hangars at the northern end of the station to the unit's dispersal.

The first American to die in the Battle of Britain was subsequently honoured with a bronze tablet in the crypt of St Paul's Cathedral, which was unveiled by the Secretary of State for Air, Sir Archibald Sinclair, on Independence Day 1941. The memorial plaque was inscribed with the words: '*An American citizen who died that England might live*'.

Operational

On the very day that 'Billy' Fiske was mortally wounded, the trio of American pilots at No 609 Sqn were declared operational. Each attached to separate sections, they would all be acting as 'weavers' behind their squadronmates on their first sortie. The importance of team work had been drilled into them since they had arrived on the unit, Sqn Ldr Darley warning them: 'If you want to go chasing DFCs all over the deck, go somewhere else. We go up as 12 and we come down as 12 – if we lose even two, the odds are shortened immediately'.

Thanks to the way Fighter Command stuck to its antiquated pre-war V-shaped Battle formation, the job of the 'weaver' was an unenviable one – and it was routinely given to the newest pilots on the squadron. Twisting like a snake behind his tightly formating numbers one and two, the 'Arse End Charlie', as his was known, was charged with protecting the rear of the unit from being 'bounced', yet there was no one in place to protect his 'rear'! As one Canadian pilot had put it at the time, 'You're either promoted from this spot – or buried'.

All three Americans survived their first operational mission, which had seen No 609 Sqn intercepting bombers sent to strike at both Middle Wallop and Tangmere. They had each fired off their allotted 2000 rounds during the fight, yet none could claim even as much as a 'damaged'. Like most fighter pilots newly arrived in the frontline, Tobin, Keough and Mamedoff still had a lot to learn about aerial gunnery, and in particular deflection shooting.

For an average pilot, his chances of downing an enemy aircraft greatly increased with every sortie he successfully completed, and even then he had to have luck on his side, being in the right place at the right time, and at the right altitude, with a fully serviceable machine. Proving this rule of experience fostering success, Carl Davis's final score of nine and one shared destroyed equalled the combined total of kills claimed by the remaining ten American pilots that saw combat during the Battle of Britain. The No 601 Sqn ace had been in action virtually from the start of the war, whilst his fellow countrymen had been thrown into combat in the deadliest skies imaginable for a fighter pilot with just a handful of hours' experience on Spitfires or Hurricanes.

By this time one of the senior hands on the squadron, Flg Off Davis continued to enjoy success through to the end of August. On the afternoon of the 18th, he intercepted the 80+ Stukas sent by the three *Gruppen* of StG 77 to hit the radar station at Poling and the airfields at Ford, Gosport and Thorney Island. The destruction of *Stukageschwader* 77 was absolute, the unit losing 17 aircraft in total. Davis was credited with one and one shared destroyed, as well as a Bf 109E (from either II./JG 2 or II./JG 27). No 601 Sqn had paid a high price for its many successes on this day, losing two sergeant pilots killed to the escorting *Emils*. Having been in the frontline since Operation *Dynamo*, the unit was now desperately in need of a rest, as Tom Moulson described in *The Flying Sword*:

'The chain of reactions from "scramble" to "pancake" which were the fabric of the pilots' lives was taking its toll of their ability to remain constantly alert and responsive to danger. During some air defence exercises held before the war, a reporter had written in an aeronautical journal: "*All the pilots were in agreement that the physical and nervous demands of these*

LEFT: No doubt in a reflective state of mind, Plt Off 'Andy' Mamedoff poses literally in the damage inflicted to his Spitfire I (L1082) on the afternoon of 24 August 1940 – the very day he celebrated his 28th birthday. Note that he has placed right leg through the gaping hole in his starboard elevator. Mamedoff's section had been 'bounced' by Bf 109s over Ryde, and he had been singled out by Hauptmann Hans-Karl Mayer, Staffelkapitän of 1./JG 53. In just a matter of seconds, the 15-kill German ace had hit the Spitfire with two 20 mm cannon shells, one of which entered the rear fuselage, took out the radio and almost penetrated the pilot's seat back armour. The second shell shredded the elevator, whilst the 7.92 mm machine gun rounds peppered the fuselage and wings.

repeated flights under combat conditions could not be maintained for longer than a week". This assessment had only been confounded by an immense effort of will, some loss of efficiency and increased fatalities.'

Since 27 May, No 601 Sqn had had nine pilots killed (including four in one sortie on 11 August) and five wounded. Short of both men and machines, the 'County of London' squadron swapped places with Debden-based No 17 Sqn on 19 August. Although still very much within No 11 Group, the Essex fighter station was then considered to be less in the frontline than Tangmere. However, within days of No 601 Sqn arriving at its new base, the *Luftwaffe* had switched its bombing attacks from airfields to London.

At the end of August, Flg Off Carl Davis was made a flight commander and awarded the DFC – he was also promoted to acting flight lieutenant. The pre-war veteran had survived 12 weeks of almost constant action, emerging as a double ace. Further west at Middle Wallop, the trio of American pilots on No 609 Sqn were beginning to wonder if they would last 12 days in the frontline.

Supermarine Spitfire I L1082 of No 609 'West Riding' Sqn, Middle Wallop, August 1940

L1082 was the very first Spitfire issued to No 609 Sqn, the fighter arriving straight from the Supermarine factory in August 1939. American Plt Off 'Andy' Mamedoff was the last to fly it, the aircraft being seriously damaged by a Bf 109E over Ryde on 24 August 1940.

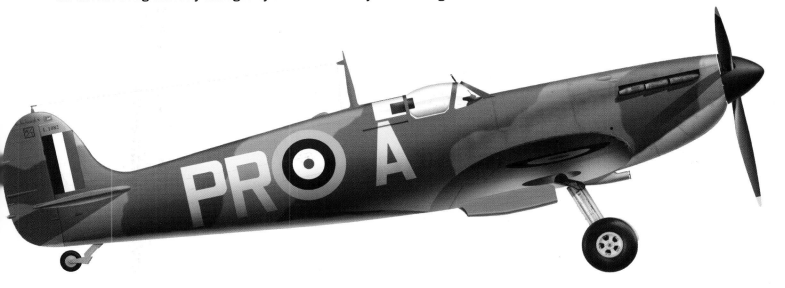

RIGHT: In this photograph, the true extent of the damage to the tail can be gauged. L1082 had been so badly shot up that its tailwheel collapsed when the fighter was gently put down at Middle Wallop. In a rare case of reverse 'Spitfire snobbery' (where Germans pilots claimed to have shot down a Supermarine fighter rather than a Hurricane, because they believed the former to be a greater prize), Mayer actually reported that his victim was a Hurricane. However, a study of combat reports for 24 August reveal that Mamedoff was attacked at exactly the same time in the same location, and there were no Hurricanes present.

LEFT: Mamedoff smiles for the camera, having stuck a finger in one of three bullet holes punched through the propeller of his fighter. L1082 was the very first Spitfire issued to No 609 Sqn, having been flown to its pre-war base at Yeadon from the Supermarine works at Woolston, Southampton, by the unit's then CO, Sqn Ldr Geoffrey Ambler, in August 1939. Note the camouflage netting hastily thrown over the forlorn Spitfire in an effort to camouflage it from attack by marauding German aircraft. The fighter remained stuck out on the airfield until its tail could be jacked up and the battle-weary warrior towed away behind a Fordson tractor. Deemed too badly damaged to repair, L1082 was struck off charge and reduced to components.

On 24 August 'Andy' Mamedoff celebrated his 28th birthday, and during the course of the afternoon *Hauptmann* Hans-Karl Mayer, *Staffelkapitän* of 1./JG 53 did his level best to make it his last. No 609 Sqn had run into a large force of 46 Ju 88s, escorted by no fewer than 302 Bf 109Es and Bf 110s, over Portsmouth. Ordered to patrol at low altitude, the Spitfire pilots were at an immediate height disadvantage of 5,000 ft, and it was only through skilled defensive flying that all 13 aircraft returned to Middle Wallop.

One machine had been badly damaged during the one-sided engagement – Spitfire I L1082, flown by Plt Off Mamedoff. The very first example of Supermarine's superlative fighter delivered to No 609 Sqn back in August 1939, the aircraft had suffered a direct hit from a 20 mm shell, as recorded in the diary of squadron rigger, Flt Sgt 'Tich' Cloves:

'A shell entered the tail of the aircraft, went straight up the fuselage, through the wireless set, just pierced the rear armour plating and presumably dented the pilot's uniform.'

Upon landing back at Middle Wallop, L1082's tail wheel had collapsed. A closer inspection

'... the shooting down here is quite good just now!'

CARL DAVIS

Officers' Mess
Royal Air Force Debden
Saffron Walden
28th August 1940

Dear John,

Thank you very much for your letter which arrived here today. I am glad you are getting some shooting. One of the things that annoys me about the war is that I have not been able to get up to Scotland this year, although the shooting down here is quite good just now!

For your ear, I have now shot down 10 German aeroplanes that I have actually seen crash and two or three others which should have crashed, but which I hadn't the time to watch. The sorts I have met are Ju 87s, Ju 88s, Me 109s and Me 110s. I have not yet met any Dorniers or Heinkels, but I expect that will happen in time.

Being in a Fighter Squadron is really a very odd business, as half the time you are bored stiff and the other half scared stiff! But having such wonderful aeroplanes makes a great difference, and you always feel that you can outfly and outshoot any German you meet when you are in them.

Our Squadron has Hurricanes and mine is now the old warrior of the flight with quite a few bullet holes in it. The only bullet that did any harm though was one through the radiator. That was done by a Ju 87 dive-bomber, but I shot him down and managed to get back to the aerodrome afterwards, so no harm came of it.

Give my love to Mummy and Daddy, and tell Mummy that Michael now weighs 11 lbs 8 oz, and is thought by both his parents to be a marvel.

With love, Raymond

ABOVE: Possibly the only photograph of Carl Raymond Davis in existence, this informal shot shows him at readiness between sorties in No 601 Sqn's dispersal area at Tangmere during the early weeks of the Battle of Britain. As the weather grew warmer, and high summer approached, pilots would often fly in just service dress trousers, a bright pale blue shirt (faded to almost white in most cases) and a black tie, with their 1932 pattern temperate life preserver, or 'Mae West', secured over the top. Standard issue 1936 pattern flying boots were also usually discarded in favour of steel-tipped, lace-up service dress shoes, as worn by Davis in this photograph.

of the damage revealed that half the starboard elevator had been shot away, and the whole aircraft had been liberally holed by 7.92 mm machine gun rounds. The veteran fighter was designated Category 3 destroyed and reduced to spare parts.

Mamedoff had failed to see his assailant during the split-second attack, *Hptm.* Mayer using his height and superior speed to telling advantage. And even if the American had spotted his enemy, there was probably little he could have done to defend himself, for the German was a skilled fighter pilot who had seen action in Spain during the Civil War – he had claimed 15 kills up to his brief encounter with Mamedoff and L1082.

Mayer had closed to within 80 ft of the Spitfire, firing 20 rounds of 20 mm ammunition and 140 rounds of 7.92 mm ammunition, and he returned to I./JG 53's Rennes base confident in the knowledge that he had just downed his 16th victim of the campaign.

The following day JG 53 again clashed with No 609 Sqn, and this time it was 'Red' Tobin's turn to cheat death. On this occasion, however, it was a mixture of faulty machinery and foolhardy recklessness on the part of the Californian which almost cost him his life. Climbing through 15,000 ft to intercept a large formation of Bf 110s, Tobin had discovered that his oxygen system was blocked. By the time he had got to 25,000 ft he began to feel decidedly odd, the brain beginning to be starved of vital oxygen. Dropping back to 19,000 ft, Tobin's head began to clear, and he was just about to ask his CO if he could return to base when he spotted Bf 110s at an identical altitude, and duly followed his squadron into battle.

Tobin fired at one *Zerstörer* and watched it dive away. He then had to avoid the fire of a second fighter behind him, before he latched onto a third Bf 110. Tobin's foe was descending rapidly in an erratic series of spins and turns, and as he banked steeply at more than 370 mph in an effort to follow his quarry, the American blacked out. His fighter fell like a stone from 18,000 ft down to just 1,000 ft above the Channel, where he came to. Collecting his wits, Tobin

ABOVE: 'Andy' Mamedoff's unseen assailant on the afternoon of 24 August was veteran fighter ace Hauptmann Hans Karl-Mayer. A man of great physical presence (he had to cram himself into the tiny cockpit of his Bf 109), Mayer was awarded the Knight's Cross on 3 September – by which time he had increased his score to 19 kills. Promoted to the position of Kommandeur of I./JG 53 at the same time, the German ace would lose his life in combat over the Channel on 17 October 1940.

flew back to Warmwell, where he found that his squadronmates had given him up for dead after witnessing his sickening spin downward towards the sea.

Newcomers

By the middle of August Fighter Command was really beginning to suffer from an acute shortage of pilots. In an effort to rectify this situation a handful of 'foreign' squadrons were declared operational, including No 1 Sqn RCAF at Croydon. The unit moved to Northolt on the day it received this momentous news (17 August), although more than a week would pass before it engaged the enemy.

No 1 Sqn's CO, Sqn Ldr McNab, was not convinced his charges were ready for the task at hand, and he was quickly proven correct on 24 August when a flight of Canadian Hurricanes downed two Coastal Command Blenheims of No 235 Sqn off Portsmouth. Three crewmen were killed in the interception, the fighter pilots mistakenly identifying the Bristol bombers as Ju 88s.

The unit finally encountered the enemy in the form of 25 Do 17Zs of KG 2, escorted by Bf 109s, on the afternoon of 26 August. More action followed five days later, and although No 1 Sqn had claimed a handful of victories by the end of the month, the unit had had one pilot killed and seven Hurricanes shot down. During the afternoon of 1 September American Otto Peterson was in the thick of the action, damaging a Do 17Z of KG 76 in an interception at 18,000 ft directly over Biggin Hill. Yet another Canadian was shot down though, Flg Off John Kerwin suffering burns prior to bailing out.

No 1 Sqn RCAF found itself short of aircrew, and a handful of newly-trained pilots arrived straight from Nos 5 and 6 OTUs, including American-born Plt Off DePeyster Brown. Little is known about this individual's pre-service years, including either his age or his place of birth. Brown joined the RCAF on 9 September 1939, and upon gaining his wings, he was posted to Britain, and No 112 Sqn RCAF. Equipped with license-built Westland Lysanders, this unit had been sent to the UK in the early spring of 1940 as one of two RCAF army co-operation squadrons assigned to a Canadian Army division committed to defending France.

When Brown arrived in the UK, No 112 Sqn RCAF had still to receive any aircraft, so he volunteered to convert onto fighters in response to a call by Fighter Command for pilots from Army Co-operation, Fleet Air Arm and Coastal Command units. Sent to No 5 OTU at RAF Aston Down on 19 August 1940, Brown arrived at No 1 Sqn RCAF on 2 September with little more than ten hours on Hurricanes in his logbook.

Also assigned to Fighter Command on this day was Plt Off Phillip Howard 'Zeke' Leckrone of Salem, Illinois. Having worked as a flying instructor in his home town, Leckrone had made the short journey across the border into Canada in July 1940, passed the RAF medical examination in Windsor, Ontario, on the 23rd of that month, and made his own way to the UK. After completing a truncated conversion onto the Spitfire with No 7 OTU at Hawarden, he received orders to report to No 616 'South Yorkshire' Sqn at Kenley. The following day the unit was posted out of No 11 Group to RAF Coltishall, in Norfolk.

No 616 Sqn had only arrived at the Surrey fighter station on 19 August, following a long spell of rest and re-equipment at RAF Leconfield, north of Hull, in the wake of its commitment to *Dynamo*. In the intervening 15 days the unit had had four pilots killed, four wounded and one made a PoW. It had also lost 13 Spitfires, including a record six aircraft (with a seventh damaged but repairable) on the afternoon of 26 August alone.

'Zeke' Leckrone's only productive engagement with the enemy during his brief spell with

ABOVE: This rare shot of Flg Off Otto John Peterson was taken soon after No 1 Sqn RCAF had arrived at Middle Wallop in late June 1940. Few photographs of the 'Canadian' American have survived.

No 616 Sqn occurred on the morning of 16 September, by which time the unit was flying from RAF Kirton-in-Lindsey, on Humberside. His section was scrambled to investigate a lone radar contact detected off the Lincolnshire coast, and after a long chase, a Ju 88A-1 of 4.(F)/122 was sighted near a convoy codenamed *PILOT*. The reconnaissance bomber then dodged in and out of a large bank of cloud that blanketed this area of the North Sea, although both Leckrone and his section leader, Flt Lt Colin MacFie, succeeded in firing fleeting bursts into their quarry.

Despite being unable to state for sure whether they had destroyed the Ju 88, the accuracy of the pilots' aim had been good, for the aircraft was subsequently reported to have crashed into the sea.

In the latter stages of the battle, 'Zeke' Leckrone and No 616 Sqn participated in several controversial 'Big Wing' sorties with the Duxford Wing, led by Sqn Ldr Douglas Bader. He failed to engage the enemy on any of these operations, however, and on 12 October the American pilot was posted to the newly-formed No 71 'Eagle' Sqn.

Yet another American pilot to take his place in No 11 Group at the start of September was Plt Off Hugh William Reilley, who for many years was recorded by historians as being a Canadian. Born in Detroit, Michigan, on 26 May 1918, his father was American and his mother Scottish. They moved 'north of the border' to London, Ontario, when Reilley was an infant, and he was placed in the care of his grandparents following the separation of his parents in the late 1920s and the death of his mother in 1930. Educated in Canada, Reilley and a friend sailed to England in May 1939, where he successfully obtained a short-service commission in the RAF the following September. He was also married within months of his arrival in the UK.

With no previous flying experience, Hugh Reilley was put through the long 'wings' course that included time at No 1 Initial Training Wing, Nos 2 and 10 Elementary Flying Training Schools and No 2 Flying Training School. Finally, in mid-August 1940 he arrived at No 7 OTU at Hawarden and converted onto Spitfires. Reilley was duly sent to No 64 Sqn on 1 September, the ex-Kenley outfit undergoing a period of rest and re-equipment at Leconfield at this time.

The unit had been replaced in No 11 Group on 3 September by No 66 Sqn, which had proceeded to lose two pilots killed and four wounded in a series of engagements over the

ABOVE: The pilot of Hurricane I V6697/ 'YO-L' taxies out from the squadron dispersal with an airman on each wingtip, heading for the grass runway at Northolt. A Gloster-built aircraft, this particular fighter had initially served with fellow Northolt-based No 303 'Polish' Sqn, before being transferred to No 1 Sqn RCAF on 16 September 1940. It was latter passed on to No 213 Sqn, and written off in a mid-air collision with Hurricane I R4109 during a mock dogfight near Castletown, in northern Scotland, on 18 March 1941.

Hawker Hurricane I V6697 of No 1 Sqn RCAF, Northolt, September 1940
Delivered new to No 303 'Polish' Sqn in early September 1940, this aircraft was passed on to fellow Northolt-based unit No 1 Sqn RCAF on the 16th of that month. V6697 flew with a primered fuselage panel on a number of missions.

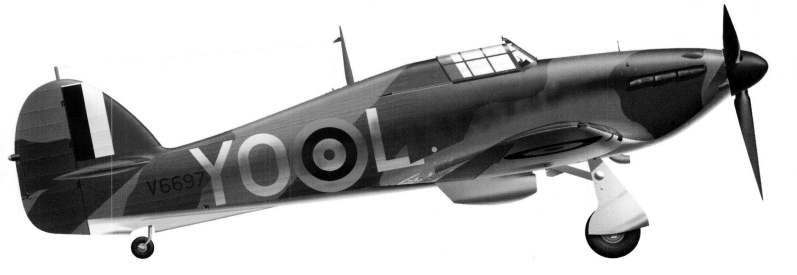

following 12 days. To make good such losses, the unit desperately needed pilots, no matter how inexperienced, and Hugh Reilley fitted the bill. He joined No 66 Sqn on 15 September – the day it was posted from Kenley to Gravesend.

Remembered as a quiet and unassuming individual, Reilley was keen for his nationality to remain a secret, and only a few close friends knew that he was actually an American rather than a Canadian. Indeed, he had used a passport from the latter country when travelling to the UK.

Bloodletting

September 1940 would not only witness the climax of the Battle of Britain, but also the high point in American participation in Fighter Command's struggle against the *Luftwaffe*.

August had seen *Adlerangriff* ('Eagle Attack') steadily wear down the resources of Nos 10 and 11 Group, as airfields and radar stations were hit day after day by vast fleets of bombers escorted by even greater numbers of fighters. Amongst the fighter stations targeted, Tangmere, Biggin Hill, Kenley, Hornchurch, Manston, North Weald and Hawkinge had been severely damaged, but more importantly, Fighter Command had lost 224 pilots killed, captured or missing since the battle had started. A further 205 had been wounded seriously enough to be taken off flying.

Just when it seemed that the RAF could no longer resist the numerically superior forces of the *Luftwaffe*, the German high command changed tactics and went after London instead. The primary reason for this switch was Hitler's rage at Berlin having been targeted for a series of modest night raids by Bomber Command. Up until 7 September he had vetoed the *Luftwaffe* from attacking the capital, but in an effort to teach the British people a lesson, he gave the green light for terror raids on London to begin.

This was the break that Fighter Command needed, as it gave its battered sector stations in the south-east a chance to effect crucial repairs. Radar sites were also brought back on line. And with London now the primary target, No 11 Group knew exactly where to position its fighters in order to maximise the damage inflicted on incoming German raids.

Three days prior to the *Luftwaffe* commencing its series of terror raids, Carl Davis had claimed his tenth, and last, kill in the shape of a Bf 110C of *Stab* III./ZG 76 downed over Worthing. The American had developed a 'taste' for the *Zerstörer* since destroying his first example on 11 July, this final Bf 110 taking his tally to five confirmed.

Davis's victory had come just 48 hours after No 601 Sqn had returned to Tangmere from its 'rest' at Debden, the unit's spell in the Essex 'backwater' of No 11 Group having seen its new home badly bombed by the *Luftwaffe* on the last day of August. With facilities at Debden in a shambolic state, the unit was posted back to Tangmere on 2 September. By now the handful of seasoned pilots that remained on the squadron were suffering from chronic fatigue, and with the rest of No 601 Sqn staffed by combat novices, the outfit was hardly fit to remain

RIGHT: An informal view of No 1 Sqn's officer corps, almost certainly photographed at Northolt soon after the unit had been declared operational in mid-August. Otto Peterson can be seen laughing second from left, whilst the short moustachioed officer in the centre of the group is the squadron CO, Sqn Ldr E A 'Ernie' McNab. Peterson was the only pilot from this group not to survive the Battle of Britain.

in the frontline. However, with the *Luftwaffe* seemingly gaining the upper hand in the battle, all available squadrons had to be thrown into the fray, and that included No 601 Sqn.

Aside from Carl Davis, fellow American Flg Off Otto Peterson also exacted a toll on the enemy on 4 September (a day which saw no fewer than 15 Bf 110s downed by half a dozen Spitfire and Hurricane squadrons) whilst flying a No 1 Sqn RCAF Hurricane I. He claimed to have damaged a 'Ju 88', but seeing that none were in the area at the time of this epic battle with the Messerschmitt fighter-bombers, his target was almost certainly a Bf 110.

On 9 September Peterson added a Bf 109E destroyed to his tally, downing the fighter after his squadron had been bounced by bomber escorts soon after it had scrambled from Northolt. The American had hit his target at extremely close range, and the *Emil* had literally blown up in front of him. His Hurricane was showered by chunks of blazing wreckage, which shattered the canopy. Peterson was struck in the face with shards of glass and perspex, cutting his forehead and causing his vision to be obscured by the blood that poured from the wound. Disorientated, and having lost control of his wildly spinning fighter, the No 1 Sqn pilot eventually succeeded in regaining level flight at 1,500 ft.

Otto Peterson had only just escaped with his life. Three days earlier, fellow countryman Carl Davis had not been so lucky.

As previously mentioned in this chapter, on 4 September the now acting Flt Lt Davis had claimed his tenth victory. The following day No 601 Sqn was informed that it was at last to receive a proper spell of rest, having been instructed to depart Tangmere on the 7th for Exeter, in No 10 Group. On the morning of the 6th its pilots scrambled for the final time from the Sussex fighter station, an incoming raid of substantial size having been detected. However, on this occasion the 'County of London' squadron was 'bounced' well short of the bombers by a large formation of Bf 109s over the Tunbridge Wells area. For some reason the 'weaver' had failed to spot the *Emils* diving from above, and in a matter of seconds four Hurricanes were hurtling earthward in flames. Two wounded pilots succeeded in baling out of their stricken fighters, but the remaining pair slammed into the ground still strapped into their respective aircraft.

One of the latter was acting Flt Lt Carl Raymond Davis, whose Hurricane (P3363, which he had used to claim his very first victory on 11 July) hit the ground inverted in the back garden of Canterbury Cottage at Matfield, near Brenchley, at 09.30 hrs. The second man to die was Flt Lt W H 'Willie' Rhodes-Moorhouse, his fighter (P8818) crashing in a high-speed dive near High Brooms viaduct, in Southborough, just seconds later.

The son of the first ever aerial Victoria Cross winner, Rhodes-Moorhouse, like Davis, was a pre-war No 601 Sqn member who had also participated in the Borkum raid of November 1939. He too was an ace, with five and four shared victories, as well as a DFC winner. And in a final coincidence, 'Willie' Rhodes-Moorhouse had been promoted to flight commander at the same time as Carl Davis.

The loss of these squadron stalwarts hit the already depleted unit very hard. The sombre mood was perfectly summed up by No 601 Sqn's Intelligence Officer, Tom Waterlow, when he

ABOVE: As with V6697, this particular fighter was part of the production batch of 500 Hurricane Is built at Hucclecote by Gloster between August 1940 and January 1941. V6609 was delivered new to No 1 Sqn on 30 August as an attrition replacement, being the last of four Hurricanes to arrive at Northolt for the unit during the last week of the month. Coded 'YO-X', it remained in the frontline until shot up by a Bf 109E east of Gravesend on the afternoon of 17 September (Hurricane I V6669 is often misquoted as having been the aircraft downed on this date). V6609's pilot, Flg Off Carl Briese, succeeded in carrying out a forced landing at High Halstow, and the fighter was duly repaired and returned to service. Parked at readiness in a corner of the airfield at Northolt during the first week of September, 'YO-X' acts as a backdrop for a photograph of Flg Offs Carl Briese and Thomas Little – the latter individual was seriously wounded in action on 11 September.

ABOVE: A pair of No 616 Sqn Spitfire Is glide in over the perimeter at Kirton-in-Lindsey after completing yet another training flight in mid-September 1940. A standard landing during this time would see the pilot fly a curved approach so as to enable him to keep the airfield in sight at all times. The canopy hood was locked open and the side door left ajar in the half-cocked position so as to

avoid the hood slamming shut in a mishap. The pilot then checked the brake pressure and extended the undercarriage, the latter only being dropped at speeds below 160 mph – two green lights and indicator bars out in the cockpit told the pilot if the wheels were down. A rich engine mixture was selected, the propeller pitch lever moved to fully fine and the flaps deployed (only below 140 mph).

With all this completed, the pilot aimed to 'fly over the hedge' at 85 mph indicated and then ease back on the stick to keep the Spitfire off the grass until its speed was down to 64 mph. The fighter would then gently stall onto the runway. Flown for the first time on the last day of August 1940, X4330 'QJ-G' was delivered to No 616 Sqn exactly a week later, and it served with the unit into 1941.

said: 'I don't enjoy my work when it entails rushing around the countryside looking at crashed aircraft and identifying my friends by the numbers on their machine guns'.

Climax

Although the leading US fighter pilot of the Battle of Britain had fallen in action just as the campaign was reaching its climax, seven of his countrymen remained in the frontline to continue the fight.

The next victory by an American was accredited to 'Red' Tobin on 15 September when he shared in the destruction of a Do 17Z of 8./KG 76 with leading No 609 Sqn ace, Flg Off John Dundas. His unit had seen little action during the near-haemorrhaging of No 11 Group that had lasted from 24 August to 6 September. In that time the 22 squadrons within this group had lost 466 aircraft destroyed or severely damaged, 103 pilots killed and 128 severely wounded.

Although performing regular patrols in defence of potential targets in No 10 Group, No 609 Sqn had not been called to assist its neighbouring units in the south-east. However, with the launch of the London offensive on 7 September, squadrons in No 10 Group were at last ordered away from their now routine patrol lines and thrown into action in defence of the capital.

LEFT: The alert section of No 616 Sqn scrambles from Kirton-in-Lindsey in mid-September 1940, the unit having been pulled out of No 11 Group earlier in the month after several weeks of heavy action from Kenley. Plt Off 'Zeke' Leckrone was posted to No 616 Sqn just as it headed north. The aircraft furthest from the camera is Spitfire I X4328, which was delivered new to the unit on 7 September and irreparably damaged in combat by a Bf 109E 19 days later.

'... he died in the air instantaneously'

ERIC HUBBARD

The following letter was written by Matfield policeman Sgt Eric Hubbard to the widow of Flt Lt Carl Davis just days after the death of the American pilot in action on 6 September 1940 over the Kentish village.

> Matfield House
> Matfield
> Kent
> 12th September 1940

Dear Mrs Davis

I hope you will not mind receiving this letter from a stranger, one who saw the air battle in which your husband gave his life on Friday morning last, his plane falling in a cottage garden within a hundred yards of this house.

I am able to tell you that he died in the air instantaneously as a result of two bullets through the brain, his machine afterwards breaking in two and falling.

I was the first to enter the cottage garden, and saw him sitting in his plane with his feet on the rudder bar and the belt still fastened round his waist, clearly showing that he had not moved again after being attacked. I placed a covering over him, and an ambulance was summoned and he was removed to the mortuary of our local hospital

His pocket book containing his identity card, a snapshot and one or two licenses was taken by the Company Commander of the Home Guard, who has forwarded it to the RAF authorities.

In order to be certain of my facts, I visited the hospital two days later, where I found him lying with a bunch of roses on his breast, and, in company with the matron, I examined his head and she agreed with me that death had been instantaneous.

As a fighter of the last war, I pay homage to a fighter of today, and while I know that nothing I may say can be of any real comfort to you, I do ask you to think of him as soaring into the sky on that glorious sunny morning, with a smile on his lips and a song in his heart, to do battle for this England of ours, and there making the supreme sacrifice.

Please believe that there is no need for you to acknowledge this letter, if you would rather not. I shall be thinking of you and him at eight o'clock tomorrow morning.

Yours sincerely,

Sergeant Eric Hubbard

ABOVE: The charred remains of Carl Davis's Hurricane I P3363 sit in the back garden of Canterbury Cottage in the village of Matfield, east of Tunbridge Wells, on the morning of 6 September. Eyewitness reports state that the flaming fighter broke in two soon after being attacked, the forward section hitting the ground inverted and then flipping over and eventually skidding to a halt right side up. The wings, engines, propeller and cockpit remained remarkably intact despite the ferocity of the fire that engulfed the stricken Hurricane, and the pilot was discovered still strapped into his seat by Police Sgt Eric Hubbard. The white area in the centre of this photo is Davis's parachute, which was deployed by the Matfield policeman upon his arrival at the scene in order to cover the remains of the dead pilot – Hubbard can be seen examining the cockpit. Flg Off Carl Raymond Davis DFC was later buried close to Tangmere in St Mary's Churchyard in Storrington, Sussex.

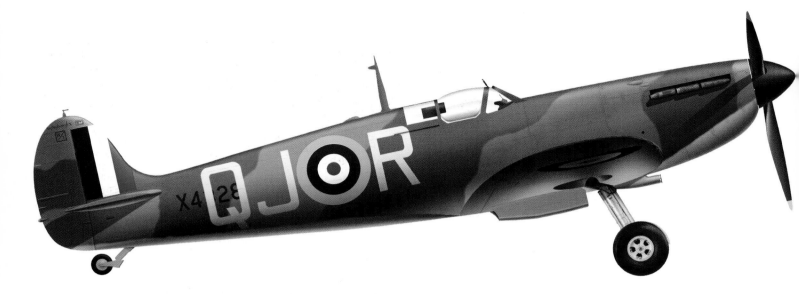

Supermarine Spitfire IA X4328 of No 616 'South Yorkshire' Sqn, Kirton-in-Lindsey, September 1940
Issued to No 616 Sqn as a combat replacement fresh from the factory on 7 September 1940, this aircraft arrived on the unit just days prior to American Plt Off 'Zeke' Leckrone. X4328 was so badly damaged in combat with a Bf 109E over Faversham on 27 September that it never flew again.

Having been credited with six victories on the 7th, the pilots of No 609 Sqn would have to wait a further eight days before being called on to defend the capital once again, and on this occasion they would participate in the most significant aerial clash of the entire Battle of Britain. Indeed, the life and death struggle that took place over south-east England, and more specifically south-east London, throughout the afternoon of Sunday, 15 September, would have great bearing on the final outcome of the Battle of Britain.

The 'West Riding' squadron claimed five victories on this momentous day, all of which were Dornier bombers. The unit was scrambled twice in defence of London as the *Luftwaffe's* supreme commander, *Reichmarschall* Herman Göring, threw every available fighter and bomber he had into the battle. Fighter Command, in turn, scrambled all the serviceable fighters it could muster within No 11 Group, supported by units from Nos 10 and 12 Groups. And at the end of

RIGHT: Plt Off 'Zeke' Leckrone in his 'office' in the autumn of 1940. The American missed out on seeing combat with the unit from Kenley by just a matter of days, although he participated in several 'Big Wing' sorties with No 616 Sqn in late September. This photograph was almost certainly taken whilst waiting at readiness at Duxford, or nearby Fowlmere, for the call to scramble the 'Big Wing', as Leckrone is sat in a No 19 Sqn Spitfire II – note the partly-visible 'QV' code below the cockpit. The fighter's toughened glass windscreen, GM 2 reflector sight, faired in rear-view mirror, headrest and canopy push-out panel can also be see in this shot.

day the RAF prevailed, downing 36 bombers and 23 fighters. Fighter Command had also suffered grave losses (64 aircraft shot down or damaged in combat), but most importantly it had shown the *Führer* that the RAF was still more than capable of defending British skies. The proposed German invasion was postponed indefinitely.

Having survived some of the fiercest fighting of the entire battle, 'Red', 'Andy' and 'Shorty' were pulled out of the frontline on 19 September and sent to the newly-formed No 71 'Eagle' Sqn. The first pilots to arrive at the unit's RAF Church Fenton base, their loss was deeply felt within No 609 Sqn, as the unit's Operational Record Book clearly reflected in its entry for the 19th:

'The three American pilots left us with evident reluctance and to our great regret. Both in the air and on the ground they had contributed colour, variety and vocabulary to the Squadron, and their "Wise cracking" will be missed.'

Lacking aircraft, equipment, squadronmates and a commanding officer, the trio of American pilots would spend the next five months away from the action as their new unit went through protracted 'growing pains'. Joining them at No 71 Sqn at the end of September was a fit again Plt Off 'Art' Donahue, and ex-No 616 Sqn Spitfire pilot 'Zeke' Leckrone arrived on the unit in mid-October.

Just as Tobin, Keough and Mamedoff were leaving the south-east, the final 'Yank' to reach Fighter Command during the Battle of Britain arrived at No 151 Sqn. Fresh-faced 19-year-old Plt Off John Kenneth Haviland joined the remnants of this battle-weary Hurricane squadron at

LEFT: Plt Off Hugh Reilley posed for this formal photograph in his newly 'winged' service dress just prior to arriving at No 64 Sqn in early September. He was posted to No 66 Sqn just days later, and served with the Gravesend-based unit until killed in action by Major Werner Mölders on 17 October.

LEFT: One of the first units in the RAF to receive the Spitfire, No 66 Sqn was kept out of No 11 Group until 3 September 1940, when it was ordered down from Coltishall to Kenley. A week later it moved to Gravesend, where this photograph was taken in the ex-civilian clubhouse. Based at the airport until 30 October, No 66 Sqn made full use of the clubhouse, which had become the resident fighter squadron's crew room in the weeks following the declaration of war. The six pilots seen wearing 'Mae Wests' in this photograph are at readiness, with the individual sat at the extreme right in a white 'prestige suit' being Hugh Reilley. Seated directly opposite the American, and leaning forward in his chair, is No 66 Sqn's CO, Sqn Ldr Rupert Leigh. Immediately to the CO's left, and without a 'Mae West', is Flg Off 'Bobby' Oxspring, whom Reilley often flew with as his 'number two'.

RIGHT: This action photograph was taken at Gravesend in late September 1940, and it shows a No 66 Sqn Spitfire coming in to land at the completion of a patrol. In the foreground is R6800, which was regularly flown by the unit's CO, Sqn Ldr Rupert 'Lucky' Leigh. He had the fighter adorned with a rarely seen pre-war rank pennant below the cockpit, as well as an insignia red propeller spinner. Leigh had ordered that the standard black spinner on R6800 be immediately repainted after he was almost shot down in error by a section of Hurricanes. He believed that any potential attacker would be so surprised by the gaudily-marked spinner that he would have a good look at his fighter prior to closing in for the kill! Parked behind R6800 is a Hurricane I of No 501 'County of Gloucester' Sqn, which also operated out of Gravesend at the time, despite technically being based at Kenley.

RAF Digby, south of Lincoln, on 23 September. No 151 Sqn had been pulled out of No 11 Group on the first day of the month, having lost virtually all of its pilots and aircraft during the bitter battles of late August.

Born in Mount Kisco, New York, in January 1921, Haviland's father was a US Navy officer and his mother English. Having spent most of his early life in England, he went to Nottingham University in 1937 and obtained his 'A' Pilot's License prior to joining the RAF Volunteer Reserve in July 1939. Called up on 1 September, Haviland completed his flying training at No 10 FTS, and then joined No 1 School of Army Co-operation at Old Sarum. He immediately answered the call for volunteers to join Fighter Command in early August, arriving at No 6 OTU at Sutton Bridge on 4 September.

The fighter pilot shortage was reaching critical levels by mid-September, and recruits were graduating from the OTUs with barely ten hours on type. This meant that pilots were arriving in the frontline woefully equipped to deal with such exacting tasks as flying battle formation, intercepting an enemy aircraft, or simply landing in bad weather. John Haviland soon realised he had a lot to learn, especially after he collided with another Hurricane during formation practice the day after he arrived on No 151 Sqn! He possessed sufficient skill, however, to carry out a forced-landing in a paddock near Waddington.

Supermarine Spitfire IA R6800 of No 66 Sqn, Gravesend, October 1940
Delivered new to No 66 Sqn on 26 July 1940, this aircraft was the designated mount of squadron CO, Sqn Ldr Rupert 'Lucky' Leigh. R6800 survived in the frontline until shot down over Crockham Hill by Major Werner Mölders on 17 October. The pilot of the Spitfire, American Plt Off Hugh Reilley, was killed.

RIGHT: A later shot in the sequence of photos taken at Gravesend sometime in September 1940. The groundcrew have now got the engine running on R6800, and its pilot (almost certainly 'Lucky' Leigh) is stood anxiously waiting for the airman to vacate the cockpit so he can strap in. This aircraft is clearly about to venture skyward on its second mission of the day, for its gun ports are missing their canvas covers and the underwing areas are streaked with gunpowder fouling. Rupert Leigh claimed two kills during the battle – a He 111 on 9 September, and a share in the destruction of a second Heinkel bomber two days later. The authenticity of these turnaround shots is lent credence by the fact that the airmen are both wearing helmets, which were only donned when enemy aircraft were reported to be in the area.

Whilst tyro fighter pilots like Plt Off Haviland came to terms with their new profession in the relative quiet of No 12 Group, back in the south-east of England, the *Luftwaffe* continued to keep the pressure on Fighter Command with a series of large raids through to the end of September. On the 25th, now battle-seasoned Flg Off Otto Peterson of No 1 Sqn RCAF was scrambled with Flg Off Dal Russel to intercept a Do 17 that had been sighted south of Tangmere. The aircraft was duly engaged and shot down near Worthing.

Two days later, on the morning of 27 September, a full strength No 1 Sqn RCAF engaged a formation of 30 Bf 110 fighter-bombers (the squadron diary erroneously identified these aircraft as Ju 88s) over north Kent. Hailing from V.(Z)/LG 1, the Messerschmitt were savaged by the Canadians, as well as several other units from No 11 Group. No fewer than 20 *Zerstörer* were lost on the 27th, which was the largest number of Bf 110s destroyed in any single day during the Battle of Britain. Five were claimed by the Canadians, including one shared by 'Blue' Section pilot Flg Off DePeyster Brown. In return, two Hurricanes force-landed and one aircraft crashed near Hever, in Kent.

The pilot of the latter fighter (P3647) was none other than Flg Off Otto Peterson, whose body was extricated from the wreckage and subsequently buried in Brookwood Military Cemetery. He was the last of three No 1 Sqn RCAF pilots to be killed during the Battle of Britain.

The unit had little time to mourn the loss of one of its most experienced pilots, however, for at noon its eight surviving Hurricanes were scrambled into action once again, although this time the unit was lucky to escape unscathed when it was 'bounced' by 20 Bf 109s near Gatwick. At 15.00 hrs the Canadians were called into action for a third time, the squadron struggling to put up six serviceable Hurricanes. Around 20 bombers (described as 'Do 215s', but almost certainly Ju 88s) were intercepted just south of London, and in the subsequent action No 1 Sqn RCAF claimed five destroyed. One of these was credited to Flg Off DePeyster Brown.

Another American heavily involved in the action of 27 September was Plt Off Hugh Reilley, whose No 66 Sqn had also been scrambled three times during the course of the day. Operating out of Gravesend, Reilley flew as the 'number two' to 'B' Flight commander, Flt Lt R W 'Bobby' Oxspring. The pair had combined to destroy a He 111H-4 of 1./KGr 126 off the Gravesend coast three days previously, and on the afternoon of the 27th both men would add single victories to their respective tallies. Oxspring, who finished the war with 13 and 1 shared destroyed to his credit, described the final engagement of the day in his autobiography *Spitfire Command*, published in 1984:

ABOVE: R6800 was also photographed after the all clear had been sounded, for its groundcrew have now dispensed with their 'tin hats'. The airman on the left appears to be checking the flight controls, for the aircraft's port aileron is in the fully up position. Note also the diamond-shaped patch of gas-sensitive paint applied to the surface of the wing. This was the very fighter that Hugh Reilley would lose his life in over the North Downs when, on 17 October, his section was bounced at high altitude by a *Schwarm* of Bf 109Es from JG 51, led by Major Werner Mölders.

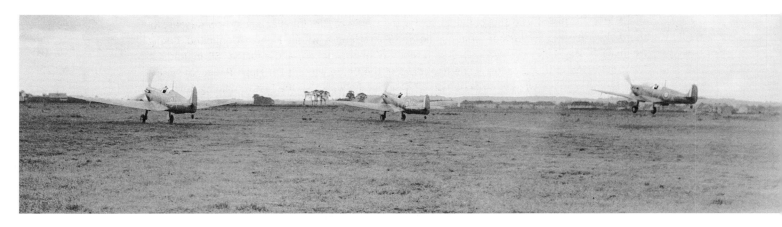

ABOVE: The alert section of No 66 Sqn scrambles from Gravesend during the Battle of Britain. The aircraft already fully airborne is N3043 'LZ-X', which served exclusively with the unit from early November 1939 through to 8 October 1940, when it was shot down by Bf 109Es over Borstal, near Rochester. N3043's pilot, Sgt Rufus Ward, was seen to bail out of the stricken fighter, but his parachute streamed and he fell to his death. He was the second No 66 Sqn pilot to be killed in action on this day, Plt Off George Corbett having been lost over Upchurch during an earlier patrol.

'Furious actions followed one after the other throughout the day and we were scrambled three times in total. Having missed our interception on the first, the second brought some hectic fighting as we ran into a formation of 88's escorted by a cloud of 109's near Ashford. As A flight fell on the 88's, a number of 109's streamed down to intercept. We in B flight turned into them and a desperate dogfight followed. We milled around snap shooting at fleeting targets interposed with savage breaks into dangerous attacks from behind. As the conflict spread and faded we hurried home to assess the damage.'

Flg Off DePeyster Brown found himself in the thick of things yet again on the last day of September when No 1 Sqn RCAF took on a formation of Bf 109Es over Surrey. His flight commander, Flt Lt Gordon McGregor, claimed one *Emil* destroyed and Brown was credited with having damaged a second fighter, although his Hurricane was in turn shot up. Suffering from malfunctioning hydraulics, the aircraft ended up on its nose upon returning to Northolt, although it pilot emerged unscathed. However, the following day DePeyster Brown succumbed to the flu bug that was rampant in the squadron, and was admitted to the hospital at RAF Northolt. He had flown his last sortie in the Battle of Britain, for on 11 October the survivors of No 1 Sqn RCAF were posted north to Prestwick, in Scotland, for a spell out of the frontline.

Little is known about DePeyster Brown's subsequent wartime career, although published sources state that he transferred to the US Army Air Forces on 25 May 1942 and failed to survive the war. The Author has been unable to trace when, where and how he died.

Freelance Skirmishing

As the weather deteriorated into October, and the threat of imminent invasion receded, so the *Luftwaffe's* tactics also changed. Vast fleets of bombers would no longer be sent over in daylight (although the night *Blitz* continued unabated well into 1941), the Germans instead relying on small formations of Ju 88s and bomb-equipped Bf 109s and 110s. These freelance missions over southern England were flown in order to entice Fighter Command into action, and thus keep up the pressure on an already battle-weary force.

BELOW LEFT: Another poorly photographed unit during the summer of 1940 was No 151 Sqn, which 19-year-old American Plt Off John Kenneth Haviland joined at RAF Digby, south of Lincoln, on 23 September. The unit had been badly mauled during the height of the Battle of Britain, and Haviland was one of a handful of replacement pilots posted in following No 151 Sqn's move to No 12 Group. This particular aircraft (V7434), seen in a blast pen at Digby, was a veteran of the battle, as was its regular pilot, New Zealander Plt Off Irving 'Black' Smith. Indeed, he used this very aeroplane to achieve ace status in the early evening of Wednesday, 2 October 1940, when he forced He 111H-5 Wk-Nr 3554 of 1./KG 53 to ditch into the surf off Chapel St Leonards, on the Lincolnshire coast. V7434's career with No 151 Sqn came to a fiery end on the night of 26 October 1940 at Digby's satellite airfield at Coleby Grange. Its pilot, Kiwi Sgt Douglas Stanley, crashed soon after taking off on a training flight, and he was pulled from the wreckage with horrific burns. He died later that same night in Lincoln County Hospital. Stanley had joined No 151 Sqn exactly a week after John Haviland.

A study of the official RAF casualty list for the Battle of Britain reveals just how successful the *Luftwaffe* was in further whittling down pilot strength within Fighter Command during October. Exactly 100 men were killed as a result of enemy action, and a further 65 injured.

Sadly, one of those to die in the final days of the battle was Plt Off Hugh Reilley of No 66 Sqn. By the time he was lost in action on 17 October, he was also the last remaining American pilot still serving in the frontline with No 11 Group. Tobin, Mamedoff, Keough, Leckrone and Donahue were all with the non-operational No 71 Sqn, Brown was in Scotland with No 1 Sqn RCAF and Haviland remained with No 151 Sqn in No 12 Group.

The pattern of fighting during October was well described by 'Bobby' Oxspring in *Spitfire Command*, the ace stating that 'the marauding fighter *staffels* were operating as hunting packs, and their formation numbers varied from half a dozen or so to *Geschwaders* of 200+'. The veteran pilots of Fighter Command were undaunted by the *Luftwaffe's* change of tactics, however, as Oxspring went on to relate. 'But we had news for them. Freed from our "backs to the wall" role against the bomber menace, we were hunting too'.

Few details exist about how Hugh Reilley died in combat on the afternoon of 17 October 1940, his Spitfire (R6800) crashing at Crockham Hill, west of Sevenoaks in Kent. His unit had been involved in near-daily high-level interceptions throughout the month, with RAF pilots usuallyfinding themselves at a tactical disadvantage as they struggled to reach the rarefied altitudes (30,000 ft) frequented by attacking Bf 109s and Bf 110s. During October No 66 Sqn would lose five pilots to 'bounces' by *Emils*, the German pilots fully exploiting their superiority in both speed and height.

One thing is known for certain about the action on the 17th. Reilley's victor was none other than Major Werner Mölders, *Geschwaderkommodore* of JG 51. The young Spitfire pilot was his 62nd victory in a tally that would eventually reach 116.

Of the 11 Americans to see action with Fighter Command between 10 July and 31 October 1940, only John Kenneth Haviland would survive to wear his Battle of Britain Clasp in peacetime. Having finished his tour with No 151 Sqn in early 1941, he instructed for a while and then returned to the frontline for a further two tours, flying intruder and bomber support mission with No 141 Sqn in Beaufighters and Mosquitos. Haviland was awarded a DFC in February 1945 and released from the RAF in December of that year.

Post-war, he moved to Canada and flew Vampires with the RCAF Reserve, before becoming a professor at the School of Engineering at the University of Virginia and being involved in work with the aerospace industry. John Haviland is still alive and well today, having recently celebrated his 80th birthday.

Hawker Hurricane I V7434 of No 151 Sqn, Digby, October 1940
This aircraft was on strength with No 151 Sqn when 19-year-old American Plt Off John Haviland was posted to RAF Digby, south of Lincoln, on 23 September 1940. A veteran of the Battle of Britain, V7434's regular pilot was New Zealander Plt Off Irving 'Black' Smith – note his Tiki emblem above the roundel.

'Eagle' Squadrons

With the Battle of Britain having reached a bloody climax just four days earlier, and the security of the nation's sovereignty still very much in the balance, on 19 September 1940 three American pilots arrived at RAF Church Fenton. They had been transferred to the Lincolnshire station from their previous home at Middle Wallop, in Hampshire, where all three men had seen action in Spitfires with No 609 Sqn. Reluctantly pulled out of the frontline, Plt Offs 'Red' Tobin, 'Shorty' Keough and 'Andy' Mamedoff were given orders to report to No 12 Group, and more specifically the newly-formed No 71 Sqn.

The arrival of the trio at Church Fenton coincided with the creation of the first 'Eagle' squadron to be formed within Fighter Command. They would be followed by a further 241 Americans keen to take the fight to the Germans prior to their country's entry into the Second World War. And of this number, 108 would not survive the war.

Tobin, Keough and Mamedoff were amongst the first group of US citizens recruited through clandestine means to serve in Europe in a squadron based loosely on the famous First World War *Lafayette Escadrille*. Keen to emulate the exploits of the Great War pilots, enjoy unlimited flying and see more action than they could possibly conceive, these young adventurers flaunted America's then tough neutrality laws and headed to war-torn Europe as fast as they could.

The man behind the recruiting drive was 30-year-old anglophile Charles Sweeny, who has been described in numerous publications as a 'well-heeled American sportsman, businessman and socialite'. A London resident for many years, he enlisted the help of his brother Robert (a successful golfer) and uncle Colonel Charles Sweeny. The latter individual was a maverick soldier of fortune who had seen action in eight wars ranging from freedom fighting in Central America to the Spanish Civil War!

Charles Sweeny's initial contribution to the defence of Britain had been the formation of the 'First American Reconnaissance (Motorised) Squadron' in the months immediately after Britain's declaration of war. Comprised entirely of Americans living and working in the UK, it was effectively a 'home guard' unit that fortunately never saw action. Sweeny then switched his efforts to forming a fighter unit to help defend Britain – continuing the Sweeny family theme, his father Robert suggested the name 'Eagle' squadron.

RIGHT: The first three 'Eagles' pose for the camera at Church Fenton in early October 1940. Plt Offs 'Red' Tobin, 'Shorty' Keough and 'Andy' Mamedoff had all been pulled out of No 609 Sqn the previous month, having fought with the unit during the Battle of Britain. Mamedoff is holding a newly-created 'Eagle' squadron patch in place on Keough's sleeve, the badges having only just arrived at the station. The creator of this distinctive emblem was co-founder of the 'Eagle' squadrons, Charles Sweeny, who used the insignia of the eagle on his US passport for inspiration. Indeed, the name 'Eagle' squadron was actually coined by Sweeny's father after he had seen the motif for the first time.

LEFT: Most of No 71 Sqn's first crop of pilots were still finishing their training when the unit was formed in early October 1940, being rushed through a truncated syllabus that saw them flying a handful of hours on Magisters, Masters and finally Hurricanes. All four of these Masters seen performing a low-level formation fly-by for the press at Sealand, south of Liverpool, in late 1940 are being flown by future 'Eagles'. Assigned to No 5 FTS, aircraft '29' (N7760), '18' (N7765) and '11' (N7691) were standard unarmed two-seat Master Is, whilst '27' (N7820) was one of a small number of Miles advanced trainers fitted with six 0.303-in machine guns and converted into single-seat 'emergency' fighters at the height of the Battle of Britain. Fortunately never needed in the frontline, they were retained within Fighter Command as aerial gunnery trainers well into 1942.

In the meantime Col Sweeny had been busy creating his own latter day *Lafayette Escadrille* through the recruitment of men keen to see action in Finland, and then France. Using his wide base of ex-military contacts to spread the word, and despite having his activities closely monitored by the FBI, the old warrior succeeded in sending 32 individuals to France between 13 April and 10 May – including Tobin, Keough and Mamedoff. None, however, saw action with the *Armée de l'Air* prior to the fall of France, and only the previously-mentioned trio from No 609 Sqn later became 'Eagles'.

With Britain now alone, Charles Sweeny presented his idea for an American volunteer squadron to his various politician friends in London, who in turn made sure that it was approved by the Air Ministry on 2 July 1940. As part of this approval process, the British government ensured that the unit was created in such a way as to not contravene the US Neutrality Act.

Sweeny knew that he would have no problem attracting recruits to his unit, for the US Army Air Corps' aviation cadet programme was heavily over-subscribed at the time, resulting in a high 'wash-out' rate. Many more potential applicants were further frustrated by the need to have

Miles Master I N7691 of No 5 FTS, Sealand, October 1940
This advanced trainer was amongst those used by the first batch of 'Eagle' squadron pilots posted to the newly-formed unit after completing their training with No 5 FTS.

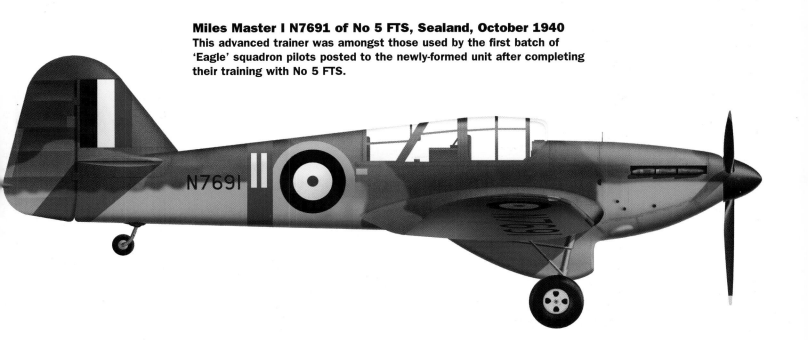

ABOVE: An instructor helps an American volunteer pilot look for the seat adjuster in a Master I during a photo shoot staged at Sealand in the autumn of 1940.

completed two years of college and possess perfect eyesight. The RAF, on the other hand, was desperate for pilots, and particularly men who already held civilian flying licences for these individuals could bypass the long elementary flying training phase and be sent straight to operational training units.

The only real obstacle facing the formation of the 'Eagle' squadron was how to fund the recruiting effort, for potential pilots had to be transported to ports in Canada for embarkation due to the neutrality act. This problem was solved by the Sweeny clan, who between them stumped up the funds (reputedly around US$100,000) required to keep the pilots salaried until they were fully enlisted in the RAF.

BELOW LEFT: Newly-winged Plt Offs 'Gus' Daymond, 'Jack' Kennerly and 'Indian Jim' Moore pose for the camera at Sealand in October 1940, this trio being amongst the eight pilots posted to Church Fenton on 7 November 1940 from No 5 FTS. Whilst Daymond and Moore would prove stalwarts of No 71 Sqn, Kennerly was most definitely the 'black sheep' of the early American volunteers. He was sent back to the USA in February 1941, having been deemed 'unsuitable' for the RAF due to a string of incidents both on the ground and in the air. Indeed, his behaviour was so bad that his CO Sqn Ldr Bill Taylor, wanted him court-martialled, but the RAF was keen to avoid any bad publicity this may have caused. Upon his return to California, Kennerly became something of a celebrity, as he spread the story that he had been sent home to recuperate from eardrum damage caused in a power-dive. He was signed up by Warner Brothers Studio to help as a technical adviser on the Ronald Reagan film 'The Flight Patrol', and in 1942 he released his autobiography 'The Eagles Roar!' Although claiming that the latter volume was a factual account of his time in the frontline, it was total fiction. After the war, Kennerly continued to lead a 'colourful' life, robbing a Los Angeles bank in 1951 and then serving time on probation. He finally died of lung cancer in a Veterans Administration hospital in California in 1967, aged just 53.

ABOVE: Sqn Ldr Bill Taylor was the first American CO of No 71 Sqn, having joined the unit from the Royal Navy upon its formation – he initially shared command responsibilities with Sqn Ldr Walter Churchill of the RAF. A serving US Marine Corps officer, Taylor had been on vacation in the UK when war was declared, and he had received permission to join the Royal Navy's Fleet Air Arm. He subsequently saw action flying from the carriers HMS Glorious and Furious during the Norwegian campaign of 1940. Something of a disciplinarian, he struggled to keep the unruly rabble that was No 71 Sqn in its early days in check. Taylor also delayed the unit's operational debut due to a paucity of pilots, which made him very unpopular with his men. He was eventually allowed to re-join the US Navy in early June 1941.

The initial batch of recruits who were attracted by the offer to fly for the RAF usually found out about the volunteer squadron through word-of-mouth via a Sweeny 'operative' at their local airport. Candidates were required to have 250 hours (later reduced to just 30) of logged flying time to their name, a current flight physical and possess a 'good character'. If these criterion were met, an interview would then take place in a secret location, where the pilot would be offered a second lieutenant's pay, possibly a commission and transportation across the Atlantic. Once signed up, the recruit was spirited north into Canada, where a flight check took place. He was then sent by train to an east coast port, and thence to the UK.

The Sweeny's direct involvement, and financing, of the recruitment of American pilots was wound up by the late summer of 1940. By then they had enough men (around 50) to man a full squadron, with a ready pool of replacement pilots. From then on, most future 'Eagles' would reach the UK via the semi-official Clayton Knight Committee, which took its name from the former-American First World War Royal Flying Corps pilot that ran it. Still others directly enlisted into the RAF or RCAF, and then succeeded in being posted to Fighter Command. However, the Sweenys will always be remembered as the founders of the 'Eagles'.

Early Frustrations

The 'Sweeny recruits' began congregating at Church Fenton in late September. Tobin, Mamedoff and Keough were quickly joined by fellow Fighter Command veterans 'Zeke' Leckrone and 'Art' Donahue, although the latter pilot's stay on No 71 Sqn would last just 25 days! On 23 October he asked to be posted back to an all-British unit due to his new squadron's total inactivity – it had just one aircraft, a Miles Magister trainer, which was unserviceable. Donahue duly returned to No 64 Sqn, and the rest of his flying career in the RAF is detailed in chapter six.

Although bereft of aircraft, No 71 Sqn had been allocated its first CO in the form of Sqn Ldr Walter Churchill, who had been decorated with both a DSO and DFC for his leadership of No 3 Sqn during the Battle of France (where he also became an ace). He later led No 605 'County of Warwick' Sqn during the summer of 1940, and was posted to No 71 Sqn on 29 September. A pre-war auxiliary pilot with considerable flying experience, 33-year-old Churchill would prove an excellent leader during his brief time with the unit.

Despite just a handful of pilots, and no fighter aircraft, the existence of No 71 'Eagle' Sqn was announced to the world's press by Air Minister Sir Archibald Sinclair on 8 October 1940. He is quoted as having said that its members 'joined spontaneously, following the glorious example set in the World War by the *Lafayette Escadrille*'. The RAF officially listed 30 American pilots on strength with No 71 Sqn at the time of the press announcement, although in reality the bulk of these men were still undergoing training at OTUs across the UK.

ABOVE: Plt Off 'Nat' Maranz trudges back to the watch office at Kirton-in-Lindsey after completing another mundane training sortie in March 1941. His mount on this occasion was one of a number of war-weary Hurricane Is supplied to the unit between November 1940 and April 1941. Unlike most other No 71 Sqn aircraft during this period, Maranz's anonymous fighter lacks the 'Eagle' squadron's distinctive 'XR' codes, which indicates that it may have just arrived on the unit. Note also the non-standard size serial partially obscured in this photograph by the tailplane.

ABOVE: Having coped with poor weather, poor aircraft and a near incessant stream of visiting VIPs and members of the press since the formation of the unit in October 1940, the 'Eagles' were itching for action by the time this group shot was taken in March 1941. All the pilots are wearing 1930 pattern 'Sidcot' flying suits, bar Sqn Ldr Taylor and Plt Off Tobin. Five of these men would not survive the war, two being killed in action and three dying on active service.

The level of flying experience amongst the men sent to No 71 Sqn varied greatly. Technically, all of these early recruits should have been able pilots with at least 250 hours of flying time. However, many had falsified their log book entries in order to reach the UK, and were now finding it difficult to transition onto the 'hot' RAF fighters then being flown within the OTUs. Despite this, none of the recruits spent longer than a month in training, for Fighter Command needed them in the frontline. Indeed, Training Command worked on the premise that it only needed to teach pupils the basics, such as aerobatics, formation flying and instrument flying, leaving the arcane art of dogfighting and aerial gunnery to the frontline unit to which the tyro fighter pilot was sent! During the summer of 1940, this basically boiled down to 'on the job training'.

Fortunately for the founder members of No 71 Sqn, they would not see action until mid-April 1941, by which time they had thoroughly familiarised themselves with the tactics associated with aerial combat on the Channel Front.

The first step towards achieving operational status came on 24 October when fighters at last arrived at Church Fenton. However, these were not Spitfires or Hurricanes as had been flown by the men either in action or in the OTUs, but rather Brewster Buffalos. Bought by the British in an effort to ease the strain on the production of locally-built fighters, the US Navy-inspired Buffalo proved a resounding failure in RAF service, as future No 71 Sqn CO, and ace, Chesley 'Pete' Peterson recounts:

'The Buffalo was considered by all of us as too slow, ceiling limited, terribly vulnerable – one bullet in the wing and the aircraft either burned or needed a new wing – with little armament, no spares and hard to maintain. In addition, the inspection doors on the wing had a nasty habit of opening in flight and making the airplane almost uncontrollable.'

Just three Buffalos were issued to the unit, and Sqn Ldr Churchill quickly realised that he had to prevent any more arriving. He therefore took the drastic measure of ordering his pilots (Mamedoff, Tobin and British flight commander, Flt Lt R C 'Wilkie' Wilkinson) to land with the tail wheels on their respective aircraft unlocked, thus allowing them to pivot. This in turn would cause the fighter to ground loop due to the Buffalo's narrowly-spaced undercarriage, the resulting 'crash' usually collapsing the undercarriage and damaging the wing and fuel tank. And with spares in such short supply, the Brewster fighter would be written off accordingly.

The startled pilots obeyed the order, and the Buffalos all duly ground looped within seconds of landing at Church Fenton. Prior to quietly ordering the elimination of the trio of Brewster fighters, Sqn Ldr Churchill had first ensured that replacement fighters in the form of Hurricane Is would be delivered to the unit within days of the Buffalos' demise. Accordingly, on 7 November nine combat-weary Hawker fighters were flown in from Gravesend by No 85 Sqn, these aircraft having served in the frontline for much of the Battle of Britain. The unit had been pulled out of No 11 Group for a rest and sent to Kirton-in-Lindsey to re-equip with newer Hurricane Is.

On the same day a further eight pilots arrived from No 5 Flying Training School, increasing the squadron's pool to virtually full strength. Two weeks later No 71 Sqn followed No 85 Sqn to Kirton-in-Lindsey, which would be its home for the next five months.

With both fighters and pilots now together at last, the unit could finally get down to some serious training that would eventually result in it being declared operational in the new year.

Tragedy

Despite having its training regularly disrupted by poor winter weather, No 71 Sqn undertook a packed programme of flying that included innumerable convoy patrols over the North Sea, air combat practice using gun cameras and formation flying. Indeed, it was whilst carrying out the latter aspect of the training regime on 5 January 1941 that the unit suffered its first fatality. 'Zeke' Leckrone's Hurricane was struck by Edwin 'Bud' Orbison's fighter at an altitude of 20,000 ft, and although the latter pilot succeeded in landing safely back at Kirton, Leckrone failed to bail out of his stricken fighter. He was followed down by his section leader, 'Shorty' Keough, who continued to shout to him over the radio until the Hurricane hit the ground.

The unit's Operational Records Book described the tragedy in the following entry:

'Zeke was quiet and reserved, and had over 100 hours on Spitfires (in 616 Squadron). He will be a great loss to us, for his influence was a sobering one. If the death of one of the pilots can help a squadron, Zeke's will help this unit for, if nothing else, it will tend to impress on the other pilots the attention they must pay to detail in these practice flights. It is true of this squadron, as of most others in the RAF, that they are inclined to treat all flying practice as a bit of a bore.'

Just 24 hours prior to Leckrone's death, No 71 Sqn had been ordered to readiness for the first time, and also flown its first 12-aircraft tactical *Balbo* formation.

Although the unit had yet to engage the enemy after almost three months of continual training, it enjoyed a tremendous reputation

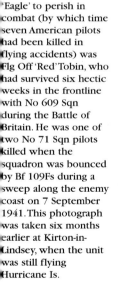

BELOW: The third 'Eagle' to perish in combat (by which time seven American pilots had been killed in flying accidents) was Flg Off 'Red' Tobin, who had survived six hectic weeks in the frontline with No 609 Sqn during the Battle of Britain. He was one of two No 71 Sqn pilots killed when the squadron was bounced by Bf 109Fs during a sweep along the enemy coast on 7 September 1941. This photograph was taken six months earlier at Kirton-in-Lindsey, when the unit was still flying Hurricane Is.

ABOVE: Californian Pole Plt Off 'Mike' Kolendorski was the first 'Eagle' killed in action – four other pilots had earlier died in flying accidents. He was shot down on 17 May 1941 by Bf 109Es from JG 53 after breaking away from his formation during No 71 Sqn's first Channel patrol. An impulsive individual who had a burning hatred of the Germans, his lack of discipline in the air directly contributed to his death. Posing for the camera in his suitably customised 'Sidcot' suit several weeks prior to his demise, Kolendorski is adjusting the straps for his parachute harness in front of one of the first Hurricanes adorned with an 'Eagle' squadron emblem.

ABOVE: On 17 March 1941 No 71 Sqn played host to an official Air Ministry photographer, who covered all aspects of the unit's daily routine. Throughout the war, fighter pilots on both sides were made to recreate a typical scramble for the camera, and in this shot a quartet of 'Eagles' dash along the well-worn perimeter track to their awaiting Hurricanes. Leading the sprint is Plt Off 'Red' Tobin, who seems to be finding the whole pantomime quite amusing – perhaps that is because he is the only one not wearing a bulky 'Sidcot' suit! Pilots who flew with No 71 Sqn during its early months have stated that these flying suits were never worn on actual operations because of their size. The three men chasing Tobin are, from left to right, Plt Offs Peter Provenzano (killed on active service in a P-47 in Alaska in 1942), Sam Mauriello (killed in an civil aircraft accident in 1950) and Luke Allen.

amongst the general populace of the UK thanks to a never-ending series of press reports on the exploits of the 'Eagle' squadron. This was succinctly summed up by American author Grover Hall in his volume *1000 Destroyed*:

'The Eagles got a reputation beyond anything accorded to the Americans who followed in American uniforms. The sight of them imparted substance to Mr Churchill's "carry on the struggle, until, in God's good time, the New World, with all its power and might, steps forth to the rescue and liberation of the Old". The Eagles became the darlings of London. They couldn't buy at pubs and got free theatre tickets.'

The routine of training flights and convoy patrols continued unabated as the winter months ground on, the unit seeing its founding CO replaced at the end of January by American Sqn Ldr W E G Taylor. No 71 Sqn flew its first operational mission on 5 February, but encountered no enemy aircraft in poor weather. Taking the form of a convoy patrol, such sorties would be flown near-daily from now on.

The continued bad weather soon revealed a fatal flaw within the 'Eagle' squadron – most of its pilots had done little blind, or instrument, flying in either the USA pre-war, or since arriving in the UK. This fundamental failure in their training manifested itself in the deaths of two 'Eagles' within days of each other during February. The first to die was Edwin 'Bud' Orbison, who became disorientated in bad weather whilst trying to find Kirton and spun in from 4,000 ft.

Six days later 'Shorty' Keough failed to return from a section scramble sent aloft to investigate a possible enemy contact. No sign of him, or his aircraft, was ever found, although a navy vessel sent to scour the area of the North Sea where his fighter was believed to have dived into the sea retrieved the tops of some size five flying boots. His fellow pilots were convinced that Keough had either suffered an attack of vertigo in cloud or forgotten to switch on his oxygen, causing him to black out as the fighters climbed to 20,000 ft.

Having suffered three fatal accidents in 40 days, No 71 Sqn came under close scrutiny by both Commander-in-Chief Fighter Command, Air Marshal Sir Sholto Douglas, and US Army Air Corps commanding general, Gen H H 'Hap' Arnold, who was on a fact finding mission to the UK at the time. Future 'Eagle Squadron' CO, and ace, Chesley 'Pete' Peterson remembers:

'We learned later that Douglas had told Gen Arnold that we were prima donnas, and that Arnold had replied that if we did not show improvement very soon, the RAF should consider releasing us and sending us home.

'Some of the fellows took a bit of umbrage at this, but I put it to them that if the Old Man thought we were prima donnas, why, let's be the best prima donnas there are. I told them this

BELOW LEFT: The weather was most kind to the 'man from the Air Ministry' when he spent the day at Kirton-in-Lindsey, and No 71 Sqn did its best to accommodate his numerous requests by carrying out as much flying as they possibly could. One of the Hurricanes sent aloft was Mk I V7608, which is seen here in the process of being started. The fighter's underside is painted in the short-lived Black and Sky scheme, which was introduced by Fighter Command on 27 November 1940. Harking back to the black and white scheme of the first months of the war, the revised finish was adopted after pilots stated that they found split underside colours the best way to locate the position of friendly fighters above them. This particular aircraft had seen action with No 253 Sqn from Kenley during the latter stages of the Battle of Britain, and was then briefly used by No 303 'Polish' Sqn, before being issued to No 71 Sqn. When the American unit received Hurricane IIAs in April 1941, V7608 was sent to No 55 OTU at RAF Usworth, south of Newcastle. The veteran fighter was finally written off when it hit the ground in bad weather near Houghton-le-Spring, in County Durham, on 15 August 1941.

ABOVE: 'Scramble' over, Luke Allen strolls down the flightline at Kirton-in-Lindsey, cigarette in mouth, with fellow 'Eagle' Plt Off Bill Nichols. The former had arrived on No 71 Sqn soon after its formation in October 1940, whilst Nichols was one of four new recruits sent to the unit in the first week of January 1941. He later became the second 'Eagle' to be made a PoW when he was shot down (in Spitfire V AB909) over Boulogne during a sweep on 7 September 1941.

was the highest compliment the commanding officer of the US Army Air Corps could pay us, because it meant that literally we were the best – and we knew it. Our performance later in the US 4th Fighter Group certainly proved that prima donnas can last out a whole war and still be the best.'

Sholto Douglas had also told Arnold that he intended to move the unit to No 11 Group so that it could at last prove its worth in combat, rather than simply as a propaganda tool. On 9 April No 71 Sqn duly received orders to fly south to Martlesham Heath, east of Ipswich, where it would be immediately thrown into action – the squadron re-equipped with the slightly more powerful Hurricane IIA within weeks of arriving in Suffolk.

On 13 April the 'Eagle' squadron encountered its first German aircraft when a three-aircraft patrol chased a snooping Ju 88 into cloud. The unit's first official ace (and the 'baby' of No 71 Sqn at just 19 years of age), Plt Off Gus Daymond, actually got to fire his guns at a Do 17 several days later, although the aircraft again got away. On 15 May James Alexander and John Flynn encountered three *Luftwaffe* fighters off Calais, and in the ensuing melee a Bf 109 was damaged. However, Flynn's Hurricane was also badly shot up, being struck around 130 times by machine gun and cannon rounds.

Due to the merry-go-round nature of the engagement, Alexander also succeeded in hitting Flynn's fighter as well as the Messerschmitt. And although the latter pilot managed to land his

LEFT: The Sky fighter band and propeller spinner were also introduced at the same time as the all-black port wing, and such was the immediacy with which all squadrons had to comply with this Air Ministry order, serials on fighters across the country were either partially or completely obliterated. Falling very much into the latter category, Hurricane I 'XR-Z' (with its codes applied in non-standard Sky, rather than regulation Medium Sea Grey) has had its serial totally covered, although squadron records indicate that this aircraft was actually V7816. Note the fighter's exhaust glare shield, which seems to have been a common feature on all 'Eagle' squadron Hurricane Is.

damaged Hurricane despite being wounded in the arm, fellow Fighter Command units lambasted No 71 Sqn for claiming one of its own for its first combat victory!

Having still to destroy a German aircraft, the 'Eagles' suffered another blow on the evening of 17 May when Flg Off S M 'Mike' Kolendorski was shot down by Bf 109Fs from JG 53 during a patrol off Clacton. A fiery Pole from California, Kolendorski had a burning hatred for the Germans which led directly to his death, as 'Pete' Peterson recounted some years later:

'Mike broke formation to go after sucker bait. It was our first time out over the Channel and the weather was cloudy. It was evident that he got trapped and shot down. We confirmed this later through German sources. He never got to use his parachute, but crashed in his plane.

Hawker Hurricane I V7816 of No 71 Sqn, Kirton-in-Lindsey, March 1941
Boasting thicker codes in a paler shade of sky rather than in regulation Medium Sea Grey, this fighter served with No 71 Sqn during the first months of the unit's existence.

'I had always said that Mike would be the first in the squadron to win the DFC, or the first to be killed. He was indeed the first Eagle to be killed by enemy action.'

On 7 June Sqn Ldr Taylor was replaced as CO of No 71 Sqn by Sqn Ldr 'Paddy' Woodhouse, who was a pre-war RAF pilot of some considerable experience. Prior to his departure, Taylor had instilled a level of operational discipline within the unit that had made him unpopular with his men, but greatly increased the professionalism of the 'Eagle' squadron in the long run.

Along with the arrival of Woodhouse came a posting further south to North Weald, on the outskirts of Greater London, where No 71 Sqn would at last be operating as part of a wing alongside two other units. The action that the 'Eagle' squadron pilots had craved for so long to legitimise their standing as fighter pilots within the RAF was now just days away.

New Squadron

Just as No 71 Sqn was encountering the enemy for the first time, on 14 May the second 'Eagle' squadron in the form of No 121 Sqn was formed at Kirton-in-Lindsey. Placed in charge of the unit was Battle of Britain ace Sqn Ldr Peter Powell, who in turn relied on two seasoned flight commanders in Flt Lts Hugh Kennard and 'Wilkie' Wilkinson (late of No 71 Sqn) to oversee the daily running of the squadron.

Unlike the first 'Eagle' squadron, No 121 Sqn took just two months to achieve operational readiness, although it too had to battle to get truly effective fighters in the form of new Hurricane IIBs in place of the 15 weary Mk Is that it had initially received. Like No 71 Sqn, the new unit also spent most of its early life performing convoy escort patrols and protecting the city of Hull.

On 2 July 1941 North Weald-based No 71 Sqn participated in its first offensive mission into 'Fortress Europe' when 12 Hurricanes were despatched as part of Circus 29. This type of operation would see a large force of fighters escorting a smaller force of bombers (in this case 12 Blenheims) sent to attack a target. Although ostensibly a bombing mission, the primary purpose of a Circus was to entice the *Luftwaffe* into action – and on 2 July that is exactly what happened.

Around 30 Bf 109s (possibly from JG 2) fell on the formation near Lille, just as the bombers had released their loads. No 71 Sqn immediately scattered, and a series of individual combats took place as the American pilots called on all their months of training to ensure their survival. During the 30-minute melee three Bf 109s were claimed to have been shot down by Sqn Ldr

ABOVE: Hard-working riggers and fitters pause for a few moments to watch a low-level 'beat-up' of No 71 Sqn's dispersal area, performed for the benefit of the camera on 17 March 1941. Although the pilots on the unit were predominantly American, all members of the groundcrew were regular RAF. 'XR-K' was yet another Hurricane I to lose its identity following the application of its fighter band. No 71 Sqn flew its 15 combat-weary fighters very hard between their arrival in November 1940 and departure in April 1941, as this machine clearly shows.

Hawker Hurricane I V7619 of No 71 Sqn, Kirton-in-Lindsey, March 1941
Issued to No 71 Sqn in November 1940, V7619 had seen combat with Nos 253 and 303 Sqns during the autumn of 1940, prior to being assigned to the American volunteer unit. The fighter was written off in a crash in April 1941, by which time it had been passed on to No 55 OTU.

RIGHT: A another low-level pass is made over Kirton-in-Lindsey, although this time Hurricane I V7619 'XR-F' is featured in the foreground. Unlike most other fighters on the unit at the time, this machine had its serial reapplied over the fighter band sometime after the latter appeared in late 1940. As with V7608, featured on page 71, V7619 had seen combat with Nos 253 and 303 Sqns during the autumn of 1940, prior to being assigned to No 71 Sqn. And in an odd twist of fate, this machine was also written off in bad weather in County Durham whilst serving with No 55 OTU – it struck a hill near Hexham on 26 April 1941. Again, the heavy level of usage experienced by these fighters during their time with No 71 Sqn is clearly revealed by the worn paint on the upper surface of 'XR-F's' port wing.

Woodhouse and Plt Offs Bill Dunn and Gus Daymond, with a fourth credited as a probable to Plt Off Bob Mannix. In return, No 71 Sqn's Plt Off Bill Hall was one of four escorting fighter pilots downed by the Germans, who also destroyed two Blenheims. Wounded in the action, Hall had succeeded in bailing out of his Hurricane and was soon captured.

For the next six weeks No 71 Sqn was in the thick of the action, its pilots claiming seven Bf 109E/Fs destroyed in a series of sweeps into France, plus a solitary Do 17Z during a convoy patrol. As with any fighter squadron, the bulk of these kills fell to a handful of pilots, and in this case it was great rivals Bill Dunn and 'Gus' Daymond. The latter pilot was feted by the press as the quintessential 'Eagle', being intelligent, articulate and handsome. A former make-up boy from Hollywood, Daymond had been credited by the senior officers within his unit as having been the first American in No 71 Sqn to down a German aircraft.

Hawker Hurricane IIA Z3781 of No 71 Sqn, North Weald, July 1941
This aircraft was used by Plt Off Bill Dunn to claim two Bf 109Fs destroyed during July 1941. Transferred to No 133 Sqn some weeks later, Z3781 was written off when it crashed on the Isle of Man on 8 October 1941, killing its pilot, Flt Lt 'Andy' Mamedoff. The 'Boxing Eagle' emblem featured at left adorned the nose of this Hurricane immediately beneath the exhaust stubs on the port side only.

LEFT: Despite having been posted into the frontline at RAF North Weald, No 71 Sqn continued to regularly host VIPs from the USA. In this shot, a clutch of pilots pose with Congressman J B Snyder, Chairman of the Military Affairs Committee in the House of Representatives, outside the unit's Ops building during a fact-finding visit in November 1941. Note the 'customised' 'Old Glory' that features the 'Eagle' squadrons' distinctive emblem. The pilots flanking this gathering in their 'Mae Wests' are standing readiness.

Hawker Hurricane IIB Z3427 of No 121 Sqn, Kirton-in-Lindsey, July 1941
No 121 Sqn's sole ace, Plt Off Seldon Edner, used this fighter to claim his unit's first aerial success when he shared in the probable destruction of a Ju 88 (with Sgt 'Jack' Mooney) off the coast of Hull on 8 August 1941.

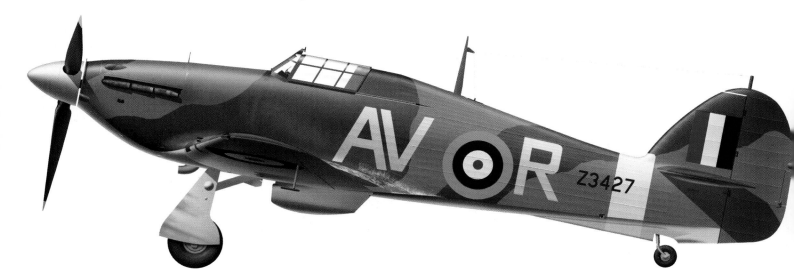

LEFT: Very few photographs exist of No 121 Sqn's Hurricanes, which the unit flew from May through to October 1941. This particular aircraft is Mk IIB Z3427, and it is seen between sorties at Kirton-in-Lindsey in mid-1941. The unit's sole ace, Plt Off Seldon Edner, used this very fighter to claim No 121 Sqn's first aerial success when he shared in the probable destruction of a Ju 88 (with Sgt 'Jack' Mooney) off the coast of Hull on 8 August 1941. This aircraft was later issued to No 257 Sqn when the American volunteer unit received Spitfire IIAs in October 1941, and it remained with the Honiley-based outfit until it was earmarked for supply to the USSR. The fighter failed to make it to the Eastern Front, however, being lost in the Barents Sea when the ship it was on was sunk by the Luftwaffe on 11 June 1942.

In fact, former North Dakota cowboy Bill Dunn had done just that, but because he was deemed to be a little 'rough around the edges', his claim to fame was pushed aside. The same thing happened several months later when it came to publicising the first American to achieve ace status within No 71 Sqn. Again, it seems likely that this was Dunn, although the propagandists at the Air Ministry officially awarded the accolade to Daymond – the former pilot's legitimate claim to this title was only officially recognised by the American Fighter Aces Association in 1967!

Such treatment rankled with the straight talking Dunn, and for decades after the war a bitter feud existed between him and Daymond surrounding these claims. Indeed, the row only really ended with the death of 'Gus' Daymond in December 1996.

Such rivalries were of no concern to No 121 Sqn, based almost 200 miles away in Lincolnshire. All its pilots were worried about was when they would get a crack at the *Luftwaffe*, and on 8 August the chance came. Future ace Plt Off Selden Edner, and Plt Off Jack Mooney, were on patrol off Hull when they were vectored onto an intruder which turned out to be a Ju 88. Attacking the bomber as it flew in and out of cloud, the Americans succeeded in hitting the aircraft but failed to see it crash, so could only claim a shared probable. Despite performing a handful of sweeps over France whilst forward-based at West Malling, in Kent, the unit would have to wait until March 1942 before it would be credited with a confirmed victory.

Eight days prior to No 121 Sqn's chance encounter over the North Sea, the third and last 'Eagle' squadron had been formed as a result of the increasing number of American pilots arriving in the UK through the highly successful Clayton Knight Committee. No 133 Sqn came into existence at Duxford on 1 August, being issued with 18 new Hurricane IIB fighters boasting

12 0.303-in machine guns apiece. Again, a British pilot in the form of Flt Lt George Brown (ex-No 71 Sqn) was placed in overall charge of the unit, although his 'B' Flight commander was very much an American – Flg Off 'Andy' Mamedoff.

Spitfires

After nine months of flying Hurricanes, No 71 Sqn became the first of the American units to receive Spitfires when 14 Mk IIAs arrived at North Weald on 20 August. None of these aircraft were brand new, however, some having seen action during the Battle of Britain, fought 12 months earlier! Having said that, they were still a great improvement over the Hurricane, and with Bf 109Fs now being encountered in great numbers over France, the American pilots needed a better fighter.

The Mk IIs would only remain on strength for a matter of weeks, and just two kills would be credited to the unit during this time – both to Bill Dunn, taking his tally to five and making him an ace. All of his successes had been against Bf 109s, and on 27 August he 'bagged' a pair of Messerschmitts whilst participating in Circus 86. This particular mission had seen more than 100 Spitfires escorting just nine Blenheims sent to bomb a steelworks in Lille.

Around 30 Bf 109Fs attacked the formation from above, and Dunn soon found himself in the thick of the action, diving after a pair of fighters as they flew through the Spitfires. Having quickly shot one down in flames, he was then fired on from behind by a third Messerschmitt, causing him to take violent evasive action. This proved so effective that the Bf 109 overshot him, presenting Dunn with an easy shot, which the American pilot took. His second victim in as many minutes tumbled earthward without a tail, streaming flame. Closing on a third *Friedrich*, Dunn had hit it with several bursts when his Spitfire was in turn rocked by an explosion. He had been hit:

Supermarine Spitfire IIA P7308 of No 71 Sqn, North Weald, August 1941
On 27 August 1941 Plt Off Bill Dunn downed two Bf 109Fs whilst flying P3708 to become No 71 Sqn's first ace. Both he and his aircraft were badly shot up in the process, Dunn never flying with the unit again. The 'Eagle' squadron emblem featured at left adorned the nose of this Spitfire immediately beneath the exhaust stubs on the port side only.

'Just as I started to press the gun button again my plane lurched sharply. I heard explosions. A ball of fire streamed through the cockpit, smashing into the instrument panel. There were two heavy blows against my right leg, and as my head snapped forward, I lost consciousness.'

The fighter began spinning wildly earthward, but Dunn quickly regained his senses and gradually pulled out in the direction of the Channel. Surveying the damage, he realised that both he and his aircraft were in bad shape. The tip of his right wing was gone, the rudder badly damaged and the right side of the instrument panel shattered. The cockpit floor was awash with blood, as the top of his right boot had been shot away, taking several toes with it, and two bullets were lodged in his right leg. Fighting nausea, Dunn contemplated bailing out, but then realised that the Spitfire's engine was still running smoothly. He opted to fly the crippled fighter back to Hawkinge instead, where he successfully landed.

Bill Dunn's injuries were so severe that he would spend three months recuperating in various RAF hospitals, and would never fly with the 'Eagles' again. His two claims from this

LEFT: Plt Off Bill Dunn is seen strapped into Spitfire I X4604 at Hawarden whilst undergoing his conversion training at No 57 OTU in August 1941. This aircraft was a presentation machine, paid for by donations from individuals, companies and countries sympathetic to the Allied cause. X4604 was one of five Spitfires 'purchased' by tea plantation owners in Ceylon for the RAF

ABOVE: No 71 Sqn flew Spitfire IIAs for less than a month, but in that time the first 'Eagle' squadron ace was crowned in this very fighter. Plt Off Bill Dunn succeeded in downing two Bf 109Fs on 27 August 1941 during Circus 86, which had seen nine Blenheims sent to attack a steelworks in Lille, escorted by more than 100 Spitfires. The American had quickly destroyed two Messerschmitts and was firing at his third when P7308 was struck a series of blows by cannon and machine gun fire from a fourth Bf 109F. Badly wounded in the leg and foot, and with his Spitfire seriously damaged, Dunn contemplated bailing out but then decided that he could make it back to England. The newly-crowned ace duly landed at Hawkinge, on the Dover coast, where this photograph was taken – notice the battle damage to the rear of the Spitfire. A veteran of the Battle of Britain with No 74 Sqn and early cross-Channel ops with No 54 Sqn, P7308 was duly patched up and converted into a Mk VA, seeing further service with Nos 133, 421, 164 and 602 Sqns, before ending its days with No 61 OTU in the summer of 1943.

LEFT: Plt Off Wendell Pendleton decorated his Spitfire with a modified version of the 'Eagle' squadron emblem. When No 71 Sqn became the 334th FS in the autumn of 1942, the newly-created unit adopted this badge as its official emblem.

RIGHT: When compared with Wendell Pendleton's 'eagle', the artwork adorning Plt Off J M 'Moe' Kelly's Spitfire V was more representative of the No 71 Sqn emblem. The latter pilot's bird of prey is gripping a Union Jack in one talon and 'Old Glory' in the other. Volunteering for service with the RAF at just 19, Kelly, of Oakland, California, was one of four 'Eagles' to later see action flying Kittyhawks with No 450 'Australian' Sqn in North Africa in 1942/43. The quartet of Americans had requested a transfer to the Far East to fight the Japanese in the China-Burma-India theatre, but got no further than Egypt!

LEFT: Another of the men to leave the UK in search of action was Plt Off 'Bob' Mannix of Daytona Beach, Florida, who bade farewell to No 71 Sqn in late September 1941. Living up to the 'war cry' (NUTS TO NAZIS) emblazoned on the back of his intricately decorated 'Mae West', Mannix had claimed two Bf 109s probably destroyed prior to his departure from North Weald. Winding up with Hurricane IIB-equipped No 127 Sqn in North Africa in mid-1942, the American saw considerable action with the unit during the great battles in western Egypt in the second half of the year, and eventually became a flight commander. At the end of October Mannix was made CO of No 33 Sqn, although his time in charge was to be short-lived, for he was shot down and killed by II./JG 27 ace, Leutnant Willi Kientsch, on 18 November whilst attacking an airfield near Mersa Matruh.

LEFT: Plt Off 'Jack' Fessler's Spitfire VB AA855 was photographed in a ploughed field outside Boulogne by a German soldier soon after it had forced-landed in France on 27 October 1941. Its pilot was something of an ace at ground strafing, having destroyed two Bf 109s at nearby airfields just a week earlier. Fessler was not so lucky on this mission, as he recalls: 'It was a dawn Rhubarb over Boulogne. I started a gentle dive at a large freight train engine in the marshalling yards at Boulogne, firing with cannon and machine guns. I continued the attack until I had to pull up to clear the engine. At that moment either the freight engine blew up, or I flew into it – I'll never know. I felt no impact, but my oil cooler and radiator cooling had both been damaged, and my engine was missing badly. I pulled up to about 2000 ft, looked for a place to land, and set down in a ploughed field just outside Boulogne. I used a post-fire to ignite my plane, then took off on foot. It was 6.15 am'.

Fessler did not get far, for he was handed over to the Germans by French gendarmes within hours of crash-landing.

mission remained 'lost' with him until weeks later, by which time 'Gus' Daymond had been officially crowned the first ace of No 71 Sqn.

Spitfire VBs began replacing the Mk IIAs in early September, and on the 4th of the month one of the first two kills credited to the new type in American hands fell to 'Gus' Daymond during the course of Circus 93. The arrival of the new fighter also coincided with No 71 Sqn suffering its worse single mission losses during its entire time with Fighter Command.

On 7 September all three units of the North Weald Wing conducted an afternoon sweep of the Boulogne area of coastal France. Only nine No 71 Sqn aircraft actually participated in the mission, however, due to various mechanical failures. This did not unduly concern the unit's new CO, Sqn Ldr Stanley Meares (again a pre-war RAF fighter pilot), for this area of France had been quiet for weeks. Additionally, with no bombers involved, the *Luftwaffe* was unlikely to be provoked into action.

LEFT: The first two 'Eagles' to be decorated with DFCs by the RAF pose for the camera whilst at readiness. Flg Off 'Gus' Daymond is sat in the cockpit of his Spitfire while Flt Lt 'Pete' Peterson stands on the fighter's wing root. The double award was announced on 5 October 1941, although by the time His Majesty King George VI came to North Weald to pin the medals to their chests the following month, Plt Off 'Red' McColpin had also been awarded the DFC.

Just as the pilots started to turn for home, having penetrated some 75 miles into enemy territory, they were informed by ground radar controllers in England that 100+ bandits had been detected between the Spitfires and the French coast. The battle which subsequently erupted was the fiercest yet fought by No 71 Sqn, for the Bf 109Fs dived on the unit from 29,000 ft, shot down three Spitfires and then climbed back up to their previous altitude, rather than diving through the remaining two squadrons.

'Pete' Peterson succeeded in destroying one of the attackers for his first kill, but this was a poor return for the loss of two men killed and a third a PoW. One of those to die was Flg Off Eugene 'Red' Tobin, his Spitfire crashing near Boulogne.

Aside from losses attributed to combat, No 71 Sqn was also suffering casualties through flying accidents, which meant that by September the unit had to call for replacements from Nos 121 and 133 Sqns. One of those to arrive from the former unit was Plt Off Carroll 'Red' McColpin, who would quickly make his mark by downing six aircraft between 21 September and 21 October. He became No 71 Sqn's third ace in the process, and would receive a DFC early in 1942 as a reward for his efforts in combat.

'Gus' Daymond was the second pilot to 'make ace' with the unit, scoring his all-important fifth victory on 19 September. However, as previously mentioned, the press dubbed him the first American ace of the Second World War! On 5 October both Daymond and 'Pete' Peterson were awarded DFCs for their actions in combat, these being the first such medals bestowed upon American fighter pilots since Flg Off Carl Davis had received his on 30 August 1940. Still recuperating in hospital in Torquay, Plt Off Bill Dunn would never be awarded a DFC by the RAF.

BELOW: Here is the third 'Eagle' recipient of the DFC being congratulated by his squadronmates on 9 November 1941. Behind Carroll McColpin is his suitably decorated Spitfire VB (AB908), which is still to be marked up with his most recent double victory success of 27 October. Achieving ace status in just six weeks, McColpin would subsequently serve with both Nos 121 and 133 Sqns, thus becoming the only pilot to see action with all three volunteer units.

LEFT: Texan Plt Off 'Jimmy' Daley poses atop his Spitfire VB at Kirton-in-Lindsey during a visit by the press on 27 November 1941. Note the white stripe painted onto the pilot's type B flying helmet, which was added to make its wearer more visible should he be forced to bail out over the sea. One of the first pilots in the unit to receive a DFC, Daley enjoyed great success throughout the spring and summer of 1942 whilst flying from bases in No 11 Group. Made 'B' Flight commander in mid June following the death of Flt Lt 'Jack' Mooney in combat, Daley eventually assumed command of No 121 Sqn just as the unit was transferred to Eighth Air Force control, where it became the 335th FS.

Last of the 'Few'

All three 'Eagle' squadrons would suffer more than their fair share of deaths due to flying accidents during their time with Fighter Command. In fact No 71 Sqn had more pilots killed in non-operational accidents (13 in total) than in combat (10), whilst No 121 Sqn had four fatalities and No 133 Sqn an even dozen. Four of those to lose their lives with the latter squadron were killed on 8 October 1941 whilst transferring from Fowlmere, in Cambridgeshire, to Eglinton, in Northern Ireland.

Fighter Command had decreed that No 133 Sqn's training effort would be better served in the less crowded skies of Northern Ireland, rather than in No 12 Group. All 15 of the unit's Hurricane IIBs departed Fowlmere safely and reached their first refuelling stop, at Sealand, less

ABOVE: In another posed shot taken on 27 November 1941, Plt Off Daley uses his hands to explain the evasive manoeuvre he had just used to get out of the gunsight of his CO, Sqn Ldr Peter Powell (to Daley's right), during a recent training flight. No 121 Sqn's Intelligence Officer, Mike Duff (in the raincoat), can be seen earnestly taking notes, whilst fellow 'Eagles' Plt Off R F 'Pat' Patterson (sat on the edge of the cockpit), Flt Lt Hugh Kennard and Plt Offs Leroy Skinner and Clarence Martin look on. Ten days after this photograph was taken, Patterson became the unit's first combat casualty when he was shot down and killed during a low-level ship-strafing mission off the Belgian coast. Leroy Skinner was also lost to the enemy on 28 April 1942, although he would spend the rest of the war as a PoW. Finally, 'Jim' Daley was killed whilst serving as deputy commander of the Thunderbolt-equipped 371st FG on 10 September 1944, his aircraft being struck by his wingman's P-47 whilst taxying at Coulommiers, in France.

than an hour later. However, soon after the unit departed for the Isle of Man a weather front moved in off the Irish Sea and only six pilots managed to make it to Andreas. Three landed at another airfield, two returned to Sealand and the remaining four crashed and were killed. Amongst the latter quartet was the newly-married Flt Lt 'Andy' Mamedoff. The last of the original 'Eagles' was gone.

Yet another training accident would rob No 71 Sqn of its last British CO, for on 15 November Sqn Ldr Stan Meares and Plt Off Ross Scarborough collided whilst flying as part of a 12-aircraft *Balbo* formation. Neither pilot succeeded in bailing out.

Their loss was greatly felt by No 71 Sqn, which had been officially declared the top unit in Fighter Command for October by the Air Ministry due its tally of nine kills (five of these were scored in one mission). With 'Pete' Peterson promoted to replace Stan Meares, No 71 Sqn became the first all-American unit within the RAF.

By January 1942 all three 'Eagle' squadrons were flying Spitfire VBs on sweeps over France. No 121 Sqn had replaced No 71 Sqn within the North Weald Wing in mid December, the latter unit returning to Martlesham Heath as part of Fighter Command's standard six month rotation policy. The unit had been scheduled to be sent north to No 12 Group, but Sqn Ldr Peterson protested directly to Sholto Douglas, who allowed the unit to remain in No 11 Group.

No 133 Sqn, however, was still very much at Kirton-in-Lindsey, although it was regularly flying across the Channel from its forward airfield at West Malling.

With the Japanese attack on the US Navy base at Pearl Harbor on 7 December 1941, the 'Eagles' realised that they had been right in joining the fight against the Axis powers in advance of the US government's unilateral declaration of war with Germany, Japan and Italy which followed the surprise raid. With America now very much in the war, it became obvious to all the 'Eagles' that their units would eventually become part of the USAAF, so within hours of the Pearl Harbor attack having been announced in Britain, they volunteered to a man to join the army air force. The pilots also requested that they be sent to Singapore to fight the Japanese, but Fighter Command was adamant that they would best serve the Allied cause by remaining in Britain.

Few kills were claimed during the early months of 1942 due to poor weather, although as early as 9 January Plt Off Bob Sprague of No 71 Sqn downed the first Fw 190 destroyed by an 'Eagle' squadron pilot during a Rhubarb along the Le Touquet coast. The new Focke-Wulf fighter would be encountered in increasing numbers as the weather slowly improved, No 121 Sqn claiming one for its first kill during a wing sweep over Calais on 23 March. On 26 April newly-promoted Flt Lt 'Red' McColpin, now with No 133 Sqn, also 'bagged' an Fw 190 to open his unit's account during a similar sortie north of Boulogne.

The following day No 71 Sqn was credited with the destruction of no fewer than five Fw 190s over St Omer whilst escorting Hurricane fighter-bombers as part of Circus 142. Although not directly assigned to a specific wing, the unit would help make up the numbers as and when required, flying with the Biggin Hill, North Weald, Hornchurch and Kenley Wings on various occasions during the first six months of 1942. 'Pete' Peterson claimed two of the Focke-Wulfs destroyed, leaving him just one short of ace status. No 71 Sqn had not escaped unscathed from its fiercest dogfight to date, however, as Plt Off John Flynn was killed in action. Just under a year earlier he had been the first 'Eagle' to be shot down when his Hurricane had been badly damaged by both enemy and friendly fire.

In the first week of May, No 71 Sqn moved to Debden and No 133 Sqn was posted to Biggin Hill. At last, all three 'Eagle' squadrons were in the frontline with No 11 Group. No 71 Sqn celebrated its arrival at its new base on 1 June by destroying two Fw 190s during a Debden Wing

BELOW: Marching along like Texas Rangers, 'Old Glory' flying proudly from the flagpole behind them, all 19 of No 121 Sqn's pilots (plus the Intelligence Officer) fan out for the camera at Kirton-in-Lindsey on 27 November 1941. At the extreme right of the shot are Plt Offs R F 'Pat' Patterson and 'Jim' Daley (with his head down), whilst in the centre are Sqn Ldr Peter Powell (with the knotted thigh straps on his 'Mae West') and Flt Lt Hugh Kennard (to the left of the CO).

ABOVE: No 71 Sqn's Plt Off 'Gene' Potter sits atop his very rare (and anonymous, thanks to the groundcrews' best efforts at concealment, which have included the employment of a blanket!) Spitfire IIB in a revetment at Debden in mid 1942. Almost identical to the Spitfire V, only a handful of Mk IIBs served with No 71 Sqn alongside the more common Mk VB. The principal difference between the two variants was that the Mk IIB used a Merlin XII engine of 1150 hp and the Mk V a Merlin 45 of 1440 hp. The only external difference between them was the small blister on the starboard side of the engine cowling immediately behind the spinner on the Mk IIB. This covered the redesigned reduction gear associated with the Merlin XII. Potter, who also served with No 121 Sqn, was killed in action over Normandy on 7 July 1944 whilst flying a P-47 with the Ninth Air Force's 368th FG.

Circus to Bruges in support of eight Hurricanes. Sqn Ldr Peterson claimed one (for his fifth kill) and Flt Lt Daymond got the second, taking his tally to six. Again, the unit suffered a pilot killed, and a second 'Eagle' was lost the following day during a search-and-rescue mission over the Channel.

More Circuses, Rhubarbs and Rodeos across the Channel into Occupied Europe were flown as the summer progressed, and on the last day of July, No 121 Sqn claimed six fighters destroyed during Circus 201 to Abbeville. The unit had tangled with Fw 190s and Bf 109Fs from JG 26, and had had one pilot killed and its CO, Ken Kennard, wounded during the dogfight which erupted over the French coast near Berck-sur-Mer. Future ace Sel Edner was credited with two of the victories, taking his tally to four.

No 133 Sqn had also been involved in this mission, but had suffered terribly at the hands of I./JG 26. Three of its pilots were killed and a fourth badly wounded when the unit was 'bounced' by about 30 fighters. In return, two Fw 190s were credited to pilots from the squadron.

Operation Jubilee

The culmination of Fighter Command's offensive campaign during the summer of 1942 came on 19 August when 48 Spitfire squadrons flew in support of the ill-fated Operation *Jubilee*, better known as the Dieppe landings.

Early on the morning of the 19th, a force of over 6000 Allied troops (primarily drawn from the Second Canadian Division and a unit of the US Rangers) was landed by ship in an effort to seize an 11-mile coastal strip of land centred on Dieppe. Their primary task was to hold the ground long enough for the numerous enemy installations in the area to be destroyed, and then they would be evacuated off the beach and returned to England. Aside from causing damage to German installations, Allied commanders hoped that the invasion would also provide them with an indicator of just how effective German defences along the Channel coast were, in light of a possible large-scale invasion at a later date.

Despite aerial support for the duration of the assault, *Jubilee* proved to be an abject failure due to landing craft being caught up in beach obstacles and troops being mown down by gun fire from heavily defended German bunkers positioned along the shoreline. Over 4200 men were killed, wounded or captured for the loss of just 590 German troops. Above the carnage on

LEFT: Bearing a squadron leader's pennant just aft of the spinner in place of an individual letter, this Spitfire VB (BM263 'MD-A') was the personal mount of No 133 Sqn CO, Sqn Ldr Eric Thomas. Aside from this highly unusual marking, the fighter also boasted an artwork in the shape of a frothing tankard (again adorned with a CO's pennant), with the legend 'MINES A BITTER', below the cockpit. A veteran of the Battle of Britain, and an ace with four and one shared kills, Thomas had been a serving officer in the RAF since 1936. Renowned for being a staunch air disciplinarian, he assumed command of the unit in November 1941, and trained his men hard. This later served them well when the unit was finally sent into action under Thomas's leadership in April 1942. BM263 was photographed at Kirton-in-Lindsey in early 1942.

the beaches the RAF faired no better, losing 108 aircraft (most of which were Spitfires). The *Luftwaffe* suffered 48 losses, including 20 fighters.

All three 'Eagle' squadrons were heavily involved in the operation, with each unit flying four separate sweeps over the invasion beaches between 04.50 and 21.00 hrs. In light of the losses suffered by other Fighter Command units on this day, Nos 71, 121 and 133 Sqns performed remarkably well, being credited with ten enemy aircraft destroyed, five probably destroyed and 12 damaged. Six Spitfires (four from No 121 Sqn and two from No 71 Sqn) were lost to *Luftwaffe* fighters, however, with a single pilot being killed and a second made a PoW. Post-war research has shown that the sole American pilot to die on this day, No 121 Sqn's Plt Off J T 'Jim' Taylor, was almost certainly killed when his Spitfire was attacked from head on by a second RAF fighter. Both machines collided and neither pilot survived.

One of those shot down was none other than Sqn Ldr 'Pete' Peterson, who was forced to take to his parachute during his third sortie of the day when his Spitfire was hit by return fire from a Ju 88 that he was attacking over the invasion fleet. Like three other 'Eagles', he was plucked from the sea by a Royal Navy vessel sailing off Dieppe. As a direct result of his inspirational leadership on this day, Peterson was subsequently awarded the only DSO

Supermarine Spitfire VB BM263 of No 133 Sqn, Biggin Hill, June 1942
Issued new to No 133 Sqn in late March 1942, this aircraft became the personal mount of squadron CO, Sqn Ldr Eric Thomas. Bearing the presentation titling *The Lord Mayor (York)* beneath the cockpit on its starboard side, BM263 was written off when it collided with another Spitfire on 19 September 1942. The fighter was serving with No 165 Sqn at the time.

RIGHT: Although of indifferent quality, this rare photograph reveals another Spitfire VB flown regularly by Sqn Ldr Thomas. BM260 'MD-C' was built virtually alongside BM263 (see previous page), the two aircraft arriving at No 5 MU from the massive Vickers-Armstrong Castle Bromwich works within two days of each other – BM263 arrived on 23 March 1942 and BM260 flew in 48 hours later. Both fighters were issued to No 131 Sqn on 12 April, BM260 being decorated with a jousting knight on horseback soon after its arrival on the unit. This photograph was taken at Biggin Hill in May 1942, the Spitfire sitting at readiness in one of the station's numerous blast pens.

presented to an American 'Eagle'. Another pilot rewarded for his bravery on the 19th was 'Gus' Daymond, who became the first 'Eagle' to receive a Bar to his DFC.

One of the two kills claimed by No 121 Sqn during *Jubilee* had fallen to the guns of Sel Edner, who downed an Fw 190 during the unit's first sortie of the day. This took his tally to five, making him the squadron's first ace. There was little celebrating back at No 121 Sqn's Southend base, however, for three pilots had been lost during the course of the mission, including Flg Off Barry Mahon, who was just one victory short of becoming an ace himself. Although the latter pilot was made a PoW and Plt Off Gene Fetrow returned to the squadron within days, Plt Off Jim Taylor was killed.

The losses at Dieppe were quickly made good, and the now familiar routine of sweeps over France continued into the autumn. By now, formal plans for the transferring of the 'Eagle' squadrons from the RAF to the USAAF's embryonic Eighth Air Force were well underway, with a hand over date set for 29 September 1942. By then No 133 Sqn had re-equipped with some of the first Spitfire IXs to reach Fighter Command, the unit being led from Biggin Hill by the redoubtable Sqn Ldr 'Red' McColpin, who had just returned from a ten-week bond drive tour of the USA. By taking command of the unit, he became the only pilot to see combat with all three 'Eagle' squadrons.

In mid-August the first B-17 Flying Fortress escort missions were flown by the 'Eagles', and these continued into September. The 'big friend, little friend' relationship did not get off to a good start, however, for the gunners in the 'heavies' would open fire at virtually any fighter they could visually acquire, be it friend or foe. Indeed, their philosophy for survival was perfectly summed up by the following phrase from a ball turret gunner quoted in a wartime Eighth Air Force booklet: 'Anything with less than four engines oughta get it!'

On more than one occasion during this period, American Spitfire pilots simply left the bombers to their fate over enemy territory after being continually fired at by bomber gunners.

As the USAAF's daylight bombing effort continued to grow in intensity, so more escort missions were being flown by Fighter Command. Sadly for the American volunteers, just such a mission would provide a tragic ending to the two-year existence of the 'Eagle' squadrons.

Despite the hand over of the trio of units to the army air force being only three days away, the routine business of daily operations could not be disrupted in the build up to the

BELOW LEFT: Fighter Command suffered heavy losses during its offensive into occupied Europe in 1941-42, and the 'Eagle' squadrons were not spared the treatment once they had been introduced to No 11 Group. On 12 May 1942 No 71 Sqn lost Plt Off Ben Mays of Wharton, Texas, during Circus 122. His squadronmate, Plt Off 'Strick' Strickland, recalls: 'As we approached the target area, the Hazebrouck marshalling yards, I noticed that Ben was more than 50 yards astern. I called for him to close up, and when I rechecked he was narrowing the gap. At about this time the two other wings with us were attacked by Me 109s and Fw 190s diving out of the sun and firing from long range. When I checked Ben again, he was gone. Somewhere well within a fraction of a second he was hit. Sprague saw smoke and a Spitfire going down. The BBC reported later that 370 RAF bombers had been over the targets on the mainland, and that two enemy aircraft had been destroyed and 11 Spitfires were missing.' Mays was killed when his Spitfire VB (AB810) was shot down near the target by veteran fighter pilot, Oberleutnant Klaus Mietusch, Staffelkapitän of Fw 190A-1-equipped 7./JG 26. The No 71 Sqn Spitfire was his 15th victory, and Mietusch went on to claim a further 60 kills before becoming the first victim of Mustang ace Lt William Beyer (of the 361st FG) on 17 September 1944.

change of commands. Therefore, on 26 September No 133 Sqn was detailed to participate in a complex mission to bomb airfields around Cherbourg, Maupertus and Morlaix/Poujean in Brittany. The 'Eagle' squadron would be providing the close escort (along with the Canadians of No 401 Sqn) for the B-17s attacking Morlaix, taking off from Bolt Head, on the Devon coast.

Following a casual briefing at the forward base, which was attended by just two pilots from No 133 Sqn, 13 Spitfires took off and headed south for their mid-Channel rendezvous with the B-17s. The unit failed to find the bombers, however, due to total cloud cover at the briefed

height and freakish high winds. The squadron, led for the first time by English flight commander Flt Lt Gordon Brettell, pressed on in search of the Fortresses that were ahead of them. The winds, blowing from the north-east, were gusting at upwards of 100 mph, and the formation was soon well out of position and radio range. Flying south-west over the Bay of Biscay towards the Spanish border, the fighters at last found the bombers as they headed back north, having jettisoned their bombs when the target could not be located. Forced to slow down and weave in order to defend the 'heavies', the Spitfire pilots proceeded to waste more precious fuel.

Having been airborne for two hours and fifteen minutes, Brettell realised that his charges would have to land very soon or crash through fuel exhaustion. He then spotted a hole in the overcast and headed down to find out where his unit was. Thinking he had returned back across the Channel and was now over the English coast, Brettell searched for a familiar landmark and headed for a nearby city, which he believed was either Southampton or Plymouth. It was, in fact, Brest, one of the most heavily defended French ports on the Brittany coast.

All ten remaining No 133 Sqn Spitfires (two had aborted after an aircraft developed engine trouble – one of these was shot down over France too) had followed Brettell through the cloud, and as they approached the 'friendly' city, they formed up on their leader at 2,500 ft. Plt Off Robert Smith later recounted:

'No self-respecting fighter squadron is going to fly over a friendly city in a loose, unimpressive formation intended to give maximum flexibility and minimum vulnerability. No way. Tighten it up! Wing to wing! Nose to tail!

'That's what we did – close formation over Brest at about 2,500 ft. What a target! Those German gunners must have had a hunded casualties, stepping on each other, trying to get off the first shot. One of them finally did.'

In the mayhem that ensued, all 11 Spitfires were shot down by either flak or Fw 190s, or a combination of both. Four pilots were killed and six made PoWs (including Gordon Brettell, who was later executed for his part in the Great Escape of March 1944), leaving just Robert Smith to successfully evade capture. The only pilot to make it back to England out of the 13 that departed

on the mission was Richard Beaty, who crash-landed his fuel starved Spitfire on the Cornish coast. He was badly injured in the process.

An investigation into this disaster found that the squadron had been the victim of abnormal weather conditions. Poor mission planning and fighter control had also played their part in this devastating blow, as had inexperienced leadership by the men in charge of both the squadron and the wing.

The remnants of No 133 Sqn joined Nos 71 and 121 Sqns at a rainy Debden airfield, in Essex, on 29 September for the handing over ceremony. By then, all of the surviving 'Eagles' had joined the USAAF, exchanging their RAF ranks for army air force equivalents. A number of British and American DFCs were also handed out on this day by Air Marshal Sir Sholto Douglas, who took the opportunity to commend the trio of units on their achievements whilst with the RAF. He commented that 73.5 German aircraft had been destroyed by the 'Eagles' in the 18 months since No 71 Sqn had become operational, and that the USAAF's gain was very much the RAF's loss. He ended with the quip, 'the loss to the *Luftwaffe* will no doubt continue as before'.

The ceremony culminated with the lowering of the RAF flag and the raising of 'Old Glory' in its place. Nos 71, 121 and 133 Sqns in turn became the 334th, 335th and 336th Fighter Squadrons of the 4th Fighter Group.

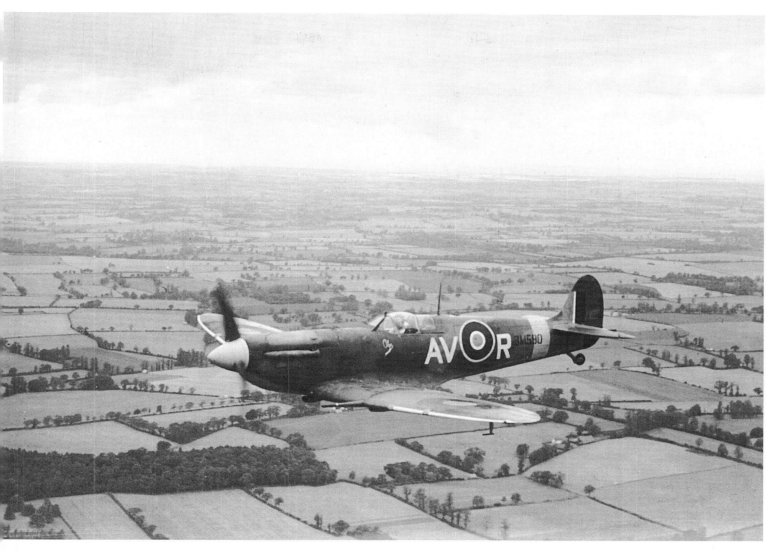

ABOVE: No 121 Sqn's Spitfire VB BM590 is seen cruising over typical English countryside during the summer of 1942. Delivered to the unit literally straight from the factory in June 1942, the aircraft was adorned with the name 'Olga' beneath its cockpit soon after arriving on No 121 Sqn. BM590 was the subject of a series of aerial photographs taken by the Air Ministry in September 1942 to help newly-arrived USAAF crews improve their aircraft recognition.

Supermarine Spitfire VB BM590 of No 121 Sqn, Southend, July 1942
This aircraft was the subject of a series of official Air Ministry recognition photographs issued to newly-arrived USAAF heavy bomber crews in the summer of 1942 to help them improve their identification skills.

RIGHT: BM590 was thoroughly worked over by the Air Ministry photographer, who had been briefed to take photos of the fighter from all possible angles. The Mk VB's underwing cannon blisters are just visible in this view, as is its radiator fairing beneath the starboard wing, oil cooler fairing to port and carburettor intake on the underfuselage centreline. This fighter was still on strength with No 133 Sqn when it was handed over to the USAAF to become the 336th FS.

ABOVE: This group photograph of ill-fated No 133 Sqn was taken at Biggin Hill on 10 June 1942, midway through the unit's first spell at Kent's premier fighter station. Standing, from left to right, are Plt Off Leonard Ryerson (killed in action on 26 September 1942), Plt Off George Middleton (shot down and captured on 26 September 1942), Plt Off Richard Beaty (injured in a crash-landing following the 26 September 1942 Morlaix mission), Flg Off Ervin Miller, Plt Off Dick Gudmundsen (killed in action on 6 September 1942), Plt Off Donald Lambert, Plt Off Donald Gentile (killed on active service on 28 January 1951), J M Emerson (Intelligence Officer), F J S Chapman (Doctor), D G Stavely-Dick (Adjutant), Flt Sgt Grant Eichar (killed in action on 31 July 1942) and Flt Sgt Chesley Robertson. Front row, from left to right, Plt Off Carter Harp (killed in action on 31 July 1942), Plt Off William Arends (killed in action on 20 June 1942), Plt Off Gilbert Omens (killed in a flying accident on 26 July 1942), Plt Off Edwin Taylor (seriously wounded in action on 31 July 1942), Flt Lt Corburn King (killed in action on 31 July 1942), Sqn Ldr Eric Thomas, Flt Lt Don Blakeslee, Plt Off George Sperry (shot down and captured on 26 September 1942), Flg Off Eric Doorly (shot down and evaded on 6 September 1942), Plt Off K K Kimbro and Plt Off William Baker (killed in action on 26 September 1942).

LEFT: Air Chief Marshal Sir Sholto Douglas, Commander-in-Chief RAF Fighter Command, addresses all three 'Eagle' squadrons at a wet and windy RAF Debden, in Essex, on 29 September 1942. This was the day that Nos 71, 121 and 133 Sqns were handed over to Eighth Air Force control to become the 334th, 335th and 336th FSs. Standing immediately behind Douglas is Maj Gen Frank O'Driscoll 'Monk' Hunter, who headed VIII Fighter Command, and to Hunter's right is Maj Gen Carl Spaatz, Commander of the Eighth Air Force. During the ceremony 'Monk' Hunter pinned the silver wings of the USAAF on all three 'Eagle' squadron COs.

BELOW: The rain lashed down throughout the ceremony at Debden, although this did not put a stop to proceedings. Here, the pilots from all three units return the salute of Sir Sholto Douglas and the various senior RAF and USAAF officers standing to attention in front of the flagpole at the fighter station. Come the end of this ceremony the 'Eagle' squadrons were no more, being replaced by the USAAF's 4th FG.

'Star-Spangled' Spitfires

The first Spitfires in the UK to see operational service wearing the US national marking were not those of the 4th Fighter Group (FG), which was created on 29 September 1942. That honour instead went to the 31st FG, which flew its first sweep over the English Channel on 26 July 1942.

Originally formed as part of the New National Defense Act promulgated in late 1939, the 31st Pursuit Group (PG), as it was then known, came into being on 1 February 1940. Staffed by a cadre of officers and men drawn from the 1st PG, and operating obsolete P-26 and P-35 fighters from bases in south-eastern USA, the group eventually received modern equipment in the form of Bell P-39 Airacobras in mid-1941. With the bombing of Pearl Harbor, the 31st was rushed to Seattle to help defend the west coast of the USA should the Japanese attempt an invasion.

When it was realised that the focus of the Japanese attacks would be in the Pacific and South-east Asia, the group was rapidly robbed of its experienced pilots, squadrons and aircraft for service in the frontline. In early 1942 the group re-equipped with P-40Bs, but pilots

RIGHT: Two members of Maj Gen 'Monk' Hunter's staff pose in front of the 31st FS's very first Spitfire during a visit by the VIII Fighter Command boss to Biggin Hill on the afternoon of 13 August 1942. The individual to the right is Maj J Francis Taylor, whilst his colleague remains unidentified. Accompanying Hunter to Kent's premier fighter station was Maj Gen Carl Spaatz, Commander of the Eighth Air Force. Both men were keen to check on the rate of progress made by the 307th FS since its arrival in the UK in early June, and to gauge the unit's state of preparedness for action.

OPPOSITE RIGHT: On 22 September the press visited the 309th FS at Westhampnett, where the unit entertained them by conducting the usual 'stunts' associated with such occasions – mock scrambles, formation take-offs, airfield 'beat-ups' and posed individual and group shots. With the scramble bell ringing in their ears, a clutch of pilots run from the dispersal hut for their Spitfires. The aircraft parked on the finger of tarmacadam behind them is Mk VB EP179, which was assigned to Maj Harrison Thyng, CO of the unit. He can be seen just sprinting past the Spitfire's fighter band. Having been credited with damaging two Fw 190s since arriving at the Sussex airfield, Thyng claimed a Ju 88 probably destroyed in EP179 on the very day this photograph was taken.

BELOW LEFT: Subtly marked with a Star of David, this Spitfire VB was the personal mount of 1Lt 'Buck' Inghram, who can be seen sat in the cockpit at Kenley in late July 1942. Assigned to the 31st FG's 308th FS, Inghram was the first of seven American pilots from the group to be shot down over Dieppe on 19 August. Flying as part of the Kenley Wing on an early morning low-level sweep over the invasion beaches, the squadron was 'bounced' by between 20 and 30 Fw 190s from II./JG 26. Inghram's Spitfire was almost certainly shot down by 4. Staffel's Oberfeldwebel Wilhelm Philipp, the American being his 19th victory out of an eventual total of 81. Parachuting down into the Channel, Inghram was eventually captured after drifting ashore in his dinghy.

complained so bitterly that P-39s were eventually reissued. In May of that year the newly-redesignated 31st FG was assigned to the fledgling Eighth Air Force, which was in the process of moving to the UK to fight in the European Theatre of Operations (ETO).

Initially, the group was due to fly its P-39s across the Atlantic to England, but the USAAF eventually realised that the Airacobra was not suited to the high level combats that characterised aerial warfare in the ETO. In one of the few examples of reverse Lend-Lease (the programme by which American military equipment was supplied to the British during the war), the 31st FG was duly equipped with Spitfire VBs soon after it had arrived in the UK on 3 June 1942.

Supermarine Spitfire VB EP179 of the 309th FS/31st FG, Westhampnett, September 1942
**The CO of the 309th FS, Maj Harrison Thyng, claimed a Ju 88 probably destroyed in this aircraft on
22 September 1942 – the very day that the unit hosted a press visit to Westhampnett. This aircraft had
previously served with Nos 111 and 71 Sqns prior to being issued to the 309th FS, and it would go on to
fly with the 334th FS and No 11 Ferry Unit, before joining the French air force in January 1945.**

ABOVE: Major Harrison Thyng is seen in a typical fighter pilot's pose whilst undertaking his conversion onto the Spitfire in late June 1942. Note that his aircraft has yet to have its RAF roundel replaced with an American star. Having joined the army as an infantryman in 1939, Thyng had subsequently gained his wings and seen service with the 1st PG prior to joining the newly-formed 31st PG in October 1940. The first CO of the 309th PS (the unit was created in January 1942 to replace the 41st PS, which had been sent to Australia to fight the Japanese as part of the 31st PG), Thyng led the squadron to the UK, and claimed its first combat successes. Claiming five kills by the time he completed his tour in mid-1943, he saw further action as CO of the P-47N-equipped 413th FG in the Pacific in 1944-45. Remaining in the regular air force post-war, and promoted to colonel, Harry Thyng went on to raise his tally of kills to ten whilst flying F-86A/E Sabres as CO of the 4th Fighter Interceptor Wing in Korea in 1951-52.

LEFT: Prior to 'scrambling' for their aircraft at Westhampnett on 22 September 1942, pilots from the 309th FS conducted a mock briefing below a rather limp 'Old Glory'. The individual pointing to the mission objective on the map is Major Harrison Thyng.

LEFT: S/Sgt Olin M Battles of Hartselle, Alabama, carries out a 60-hour inspection on a 309th FS Spitfire VB in one of the temporary Miskin steel blister hangars erected at Westhampnett. Like most Supermarine fighters assigned to the 31st FG in Britain, this aircraft has been personalised through the addition of a nickname below the windscreen.

BELOW: In late August 1942 the 308th FS was also posted to Westhampnett from Kenley, thus allowing the 31st FG to operate more as a group. This photograph of the squadron's 'B' Flight was taken at the Sussex base during September. The pilot at the extreme right of the shot is 1Lt Frank Hill, who would later become the group's top-scoring Spitfire ace with seven kills, two probables and five damaged (all bar a single probable being claimed in the Mediterranean theatre). He also lead the 308th and 309th FSs prior to assuming command of the group in mid-July 1943.

Based at Atcham, in Shropshire, the group got down to the serious business of learning to operate a totally new type of fighter after having flown P-39s for over a year. One of the first things to be done was to paint out the RAF roundel with a US white star on a blue disc. The fin flash was also deleted, although RAF fighter codes were adopted, with the 307th FS using 'MX', the 308th 'HL' and the 309th 'WZ'. These would remain unchanged until war's end.

Pilots had to get used to the Spitfire's narrow undercarriage, non-steerable tailwheel and

LEFT: 1Lt Frank Hill's Spitfire VB is seen airborne on a convoy patrol over the Channel during the summer of 1942, the fighter being flown by 1Lt Edward Dalrymple on this occasion. Note that the Spitfire is fitted with a blunt de Havilland propeller spinner rather than the more common Rotol. The former was almost a 'standard fit' on early marks of Spitfire, which suggest that this particular machine may have been a converted Mk I or II.

poor brakes, as well as a spade-shaped control column grip (the P-39's was in the standard American pistol grip style) and no aileron trim tabs. The weather was also vastly different to that typically encountered in the US, as was the geography of England.

Faced with such obstacles, and under pressure to attain operational status as soon as possible, the 31st FG inevitably suffered its fair share of accidents. On 28 June alone, four aircraft were written off in crashes, whilst the following day the group had its first pilot killed during a training flight. By 14 July 21 aircraft had been either written off or badly damaged in just 16 days of flying, and the group was urged to take a more cautious approach to its training!

Twelve days later the 31st got to participate in its first sortie when the group's Executive Officer, Lt Col Albert Clark, and five other pilots from the 308th FS accompanied No 412 'Canadian' Sqn on a sweep from Biggin Hill. After strafing the *Luftwaffe* base at Abbeville, the Spitfires were attacked by fighters, and Lt Col Clark was shot down by *Leutnant* Heinz Rahardt, flying a Fw 190A-2 of 2./JG 26. The American survived to become a PoW, and in a strange twist of fate, Rahardt was in turn shot down and killed by Flt Lt Don Blakeslee of No 133 'Eagle' Sqn during a sweep on 18 August 1942.

This early loss of Lt Col Clark did not prevent the 31st FG from being declared operational, and it duly moved south-east from Atcham into the frontline. In order to gain further experience, all three units were attached to an RAF wing, the 307th FS going to Biggin Hill, the 308th to Kenley and the 309th to Westhampnett. The squadrons arrived on 1 August, and five days later

Supermarine Spitfire VB (serial unknown) of the 308th FS/31st FG, Kenley, August 1942
Fitted with a blunt de Havilland propeller spinner rather than the more common Rotol, this aircraft was the mount of 1Lt Frank Hill, who later became the 31st FG's most successful Spitfire ace in the MTO.

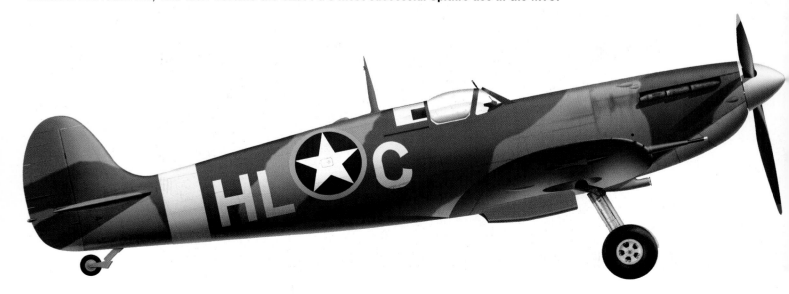

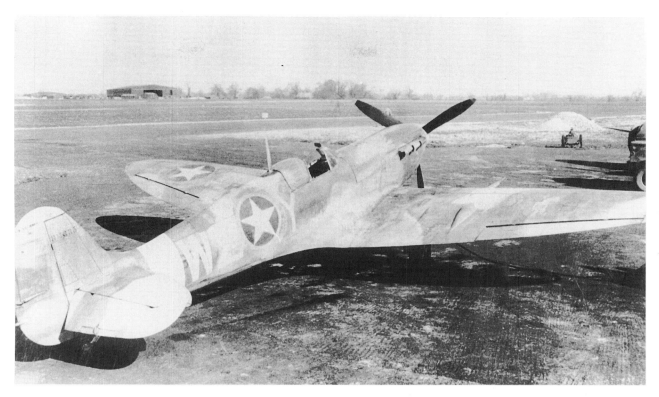

ABOVE AND LEFT: Spitfire VB BM635 was amongst the batch of new aircraft delivered to RAF High Ercall, in Shropshire, on 21 June 1942 for use by the 31st FG upon the group's arrival in the UK. Slightly damaged in a flying accident on 20 July, it remained with the 309th FS until the unit was sent to North Africa with the rest of the 31st FG. As these photographs clearly reveals, BM635 was well used during its time with the Americans, the aircraft's Day Fighter Scheme looking decidedly the worst for wear by the autumn of 1942. Following repainting, it was issued to No 65 Sqn at RAF Drem in early December, where it stayed until sent to de Havilland for a major overhaul 11 months later. The veteran fighter returned to Shropshire to finish its service career in late September 1944, flying with No 61 OTU at Rednal until it was struck off charge in February 1945.

1Lts E S Schofield (left) and R F Sargent enjoy a cigarette between flights at an unidentified airfield (possibly Debden) in early October 1942. The former is wearing an RAF issue type C-2 seat pack parachute over his standard USAAF A-4 summer suit. His squadronmate, however, appears to have on RAF battledress, over which he is wearing a bulky Thermally Insulated Flying Jacket, better known as an Irvin jacket. Sargent's footwear is also of British origin in the form of 1941 pattern flying boots. The well-weathered Spitfire bears both the 'MX' codes and squadron badge of the 307th FS.

two 309th FS Spitfires on a gunnery practice flight were scrambled after a lone Fw 190 fighter-bomber detected over Shoreham, on the Sussex coast. Flying one of the Spitfires was squadron CO, Maj Harrison Thyng, who fired at the fleeing Focke-Wulf and claimed to have damaged it. Other Fw 190s were detected in the area, but none were encountered.

Over the next nine days the various units flew both Rodeos and sweeps into France, with few enemy aircraft being encountered. This would all change on 19 August.

Operation Jubilee

Such were the strides made by the 31st FG since achieving operational status in early August that the group became the only USAAF fighter outfit to participate in Operation *Jubilee* on 19 August 1942.

As detailed in chapter four, the Allies attempted to land a large commando force on the Dieppe beaches in an effort to destroy various enemy coastal installations. Fighter Command was charged with seizing aerial supremacy over the French town, and to that end 48 Spitfire squadrons were committed to the operation. Playing its part, the 31st's trio of units completed 11 missions between them, destroying two Fw 190s, probably destroying three more and damaging two fighters and a Do 217. In return, the group suffered three of its pilots killed, one captured and one seriously wounded, all of these casualties being inflicted by the Fw 190s of 4./JG 26.

The 31st FG would remain in the frontline in south-east England until October, when it was transferred to the newly-created Twelfth Air Force and readied for movement to North Africa to help support Operation *Torch* (the Anglo-American invasion of North Africa, launched in November 1942). During its final weeks in the UK, the group had flown more sweeps over France, and escorted Eighth Air Force B-17s on some of the first daylight bombing raids performed by the USAAF in the ETO. In an effort to facilitate wing-strength operations, all three units had been concentrated on the Sussex coast at Merston (307th FS) and Westhampnett (308th and 309th FSs) in late August, and on the 29th of that month the 31st FG flew its first mission as a group.

The 31st would suffer no further operational losses following the Dieppe raid, and only claim a single Ju 88 probably destroyed, on 22 September (again credited to Maj Thyng). The group had by then flown its last operational mission into France with the Eighth Air Force, escorting 12 A-20s sent to bomb Le Havre on 5 September.

Declared non-operational on 13 October, the 31st FG spent the rest of its time in the UK preparing for the move to North Africa.

Supermarine Spitfire VC EN851 of the 307th FS/31st FG, Merston, September 1942
Bearing the presentation titling *LIMA CHALLENGER* forward of the cockpit, EN851 had been 'gifted' to the RAF by Mr H L Woodhouse of Lima, Peru. Following service with the 31st FG, it was converted into a Seafire IB (NX952) by Cunliffe Owen Aircraft Ltd in late 1943. The official 307th FS emblem featured below left adorned the cockpit hatch of most Spitfires flown by this unit in 1942, including EN851.

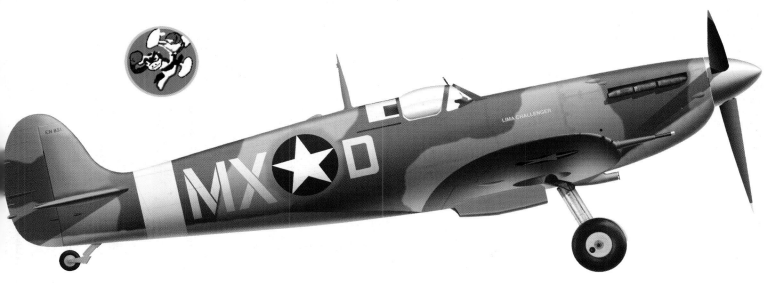

LEFT: A 308th FS Spitfire VB is serviced between flights at Westhampnett on 3 September 1942. One groundcrewman is refilling the fighter's 48-gallon main fuselage fuel tank from a nearby bowser, another is giving the blown canopy a good polish and a third individual is checking the frequency settings for the aircraft's transmitter/ receiver, installed in its own compartment below the aerial mast. The constant repetition of this procedure soon revealed the bare metal of the Spitfire's wing root, which has been inexplicably touched up with insignia white paint in this particular instance.

RIGHT: With the formation of the 4th FG in late September 1942, a seasoned RAF officer in the form of Wg Cdr Myles Duke-Woolley was given command of the group when airborne. A pre-war pilot who had seen action in Blenheim nightfighters and then in Hurricanes during the Battle of Britain, the 'Dook', as he was known to his American charges, served as Debden 'wingco' in the months prior to the formation of the 4th FG. An ace with four and three shared kills, Duke-Woolley was the first non-American pilot to be awarded a US DFC, which he wore alongside a British DFC and Bar, as well as a DSO. Working closely with VIII Fighter Command, he had a unique insight into the psyche of the average American combat pilot, as he recounted in 'Jim' Goodson's 'Over-Paid, Over-Sexed and Over Here'. 'I got on with the Americans very well, but tactically speaking they were a little impetuous, wanting the war won the day after tomorrow, which was a most dangerous thing to do, and in any case, totally unnecessary. We were in for a five- or six-year war, and so to go blazing around trying to win it by Wednesday week was not on'.

RIGHT: The home for the 4th FG from its inception to war's end was RAF Debden, in Essex. This aerial view of the fighter station was taken in late 1944, although the main hangars and general layout of the site had changed little from when the 'Eagle' squadrons became the 4th FG on 29 September 1942. The parade ground on which the rain-swept handing over ceremony took place can be seen in the right foreground of this photograph. Built between 1935 and 1939, Debden was a sector station for Fighter Command's No 11 Group during the Battle of Britain, and became home for the Debden Wing until turned over to the US authorities for use by the Eighth Air Force. This shot clearly reveals how the airfield was dominated by three 152-ft span C-type hangars, with two intersecting runways of 1600 and 1300 yards visible in the distance . Other aircraft can also be seen dispersed along the perimeter track that runs around the edge of the airfield – particularly in front of Abbotts Farm, which continues up to the runways' point of intersection.

52nd Fighter Group

Following very much in the footsteps of the 31st FG was the 52nd FG, which was formed as the 52nd PG on 15 January 1941. Initially staffed by pilots and groundcrews pulled from the 1st and 31st PGs, the group's three units (2nd, 4th and 5th PSs) worked up on a mixed fleet of obsolescent P-35s, P-36s and P-43s in Michigan until finally issued with P-39s in January 1942.

As with the 31st FG, the 52nd received orders assigning it to the Eighth Air Force in May 1942, and like the former unit, the group left its P-39s behind when it sailed for the UK on 1 July. Posted to Eglinton, in Northern Ireland, upon its arrival in the ETO, the 31st soon commenced its conversion onto the Spitfire VB. The group would stay in Northern Ireland until late August, flying convoy patrols along the Atlantic coast and over the Irish Sea. On the 19th of that month, two aircraft were sent to intercept an enemy aircraft detected off Northern Ireland, but nothing was found. The 52nd FG had recorded it first operational sorties in the process, however.

After completing their training, the group's 2nd and 4th FSs were sent to Biggin Hill and Kenley, respectively, during the first week of September, whilst the 5th FS remained at Eglinton continuing its conversion – the latter unit never flew actual combat operations from the UK. On the 7th the 2nd FS undertook its first sweep along the French coast, and the squadron CO, Capt R E Keyes, was pleased to report during the mission debrief that his charges 'didn't get lost' whilst watching a top cover Canadian unit engage the *Luftwaffe* above them.

RIGHT: 4th FG CO Lt Col Chesley 'Pete' Peterson was just one of a number of pilots that participated in a press photographic session staged at Debden in late March 1943. The group's Spitfires also featured prominently on the day, despite them having been taken off offensive operations whilst the 4th transitioned onto the P-47. The USAAF was keen to create the impression that the Supermarine fighter was still in active use, and thus trick enemy intelligence into believing that American Spitfires remained a part of the frontline force.

RIGHT: This heavily censored photograph shows Spitfire VB EN783 at Debden (the control tower has been officially removed from the background) in late 1942. Wearing 334th FS 'XR' codes, this fighter had been on strength with No 71 Sqn when the 'Eagle' squadrons became the 4th FG in late September 1942. A much-travelled aircraft, it had originally been delivered new to No 610 Sqn on 21 May 1942, but was then passed on to the 31st FG's 308th FS on 15 July. EN783 remained within the group when it was issued to the 309th FS on 24 August, and the unit in turn sent it to No 71 Sqn 19 days later. Re-engined with a Merlin 46 and mechanically upgraded by Vickers-Supermarine once declared surplus to requirements by the 4th FG in March 1943, the aircraft saw fleeting frontline service with Nos 66 and 340 Sqns eight months later. Damaged in combat on 7 December, EN783 was duly repaired and sent to No 1 Tactical Exercise Unit (TEU) on 16 June 1944, followed by No 57 OTU on 12 September. The veteran fighter was finally written off on 2 May 1945 when engine failure caused its pilot to crash-land in a field near Eshott, in Northumberland.

Supermarine Spitfire VB EN783 of the 334th FS/4th FG, Debden, October 1942
An ex-No 71 Sqn aircraft, EN783 went on to serve with the 31st FG, before being returned to RAF control in the spring of 1943. It saw further frontline action with Nos 66 and 340 Sqns, and was eventually written off in a crash-landing on 2 May 1945.

A second sweep was carried out by 11 Spitfires from the Kenley-based 4th FS on 10 September, but again no German aircraft were encountered. In the middle of the month 22 former 'Eagle' squadron pilots were transferred into the group, by which time all three units had been consolidated at RAF Goxhill, in Lincolnshire. As with the 31st FG, the 52nd was assigned to the newly-created Twelfth Air Force and despatched to North Africa for Operation *Torch* on 1 November 1942.

4th Fighter Group

The large-scale invasion of North Africa had effectively denuded the Eighth Air Force of virtually all of its fighter strength and much of its heavy bomber force. Indeed, of the four fighter groups deemed operational within VIII Fighter Command on 1 October 1942, only the 4th FG was still assigned to the Eighth come the end of the month.

Despite having lost three-quarters of its pilots, the Eighth Air Force was fortunate to have retained the services of the most experienced American aviators in the ETO, and these men would help VIII Fighter Command rapidly restore itself to full strength.

Based at Debden, and staffed by the combat veterans of the former 'Eagle' squadrons, the 4th FG operated in a similar fashion to any other wing within RAF Fighter Command during the

BELOW: An unidentified pilot poses on the wing of a 334th FS Spitfire VB at Debden, whilst his equally anonymous squadronmate extricates himself from the fighter's cockpit. Note how exhaust-streaked and chipped the paintwork is, and that both the undercarriage legs and the radiator fairing are caked in dried mud.

RIGHT: 'AV-V' of the 335th FS appears to be suffering from some kind of oil or glycol leak judging by the large puddle of liquid forming beneath its engine. Photographed within one of the many blast pens scattered around the perimeter track at Debden in February 1943, this aircraft sits opposite a clipped-wing Spitfire VB of the 336th FS.

BELOW RIGHT: Spitfire VB EN853 was the personal mount of the 335th FS's first CO, Major 'Jim' Daley, until he returned to the US tour-expired on 22 November 1942. His final claim in the ETO was almost certainly achieved in this aircraft, Daley being credited with damaging an Fw 190 east of Calais whilst leading his unit on an escort mission for a diversionary bombing force from the Eighth Air Force. Yet another aircraft previously on strength with an 'Eagle' squadron at the time of the hand over to the USAAF, EN853 had initially seen frontline service with No 401 'Canadian' Sqn from 4 June 1942 through to 5 August, when it was passed on to No 121 Sqn. The aircraft was subsequently shot down by flak whilst escorting RAF Bostons sent to bomb the airfield at St Omer on the afternoon of 22 January 1943. Its pilot, 2Lt Chester Grimm, was seen to bail out of the stricken Spitfire off Dunkirk, but his body was never found.

first months of its existence. Indeed, the RAF referred to the group as the 'Debden Wing' until well into 1943, the outfit being commanded on the ground by an American (Col Edward Anderson) and in the air by an RAF officer (Wg Cdr Raymond Duke-Woolley). Finally, operational control of the group remained with the British until June of the following year.

Although the former volunteer pilots of the new 4th FG would take time to adjust to the USAAF's more formal rules and regulations, one of the first changes to take place at Debden was the adoption of the American star in place of the RAF roundel. Ex-No 133 Sqn pilot 'Jim' Goodson remembers:

'Dixie Alexander and I badgered Don Blakeslee to let us do a Rhubarb over France and we eventually got permission – provided we painted over the RAF roundel with the American star. I don't know if you have ever tried to draw a five-pointed star, but it's not easy. Eventually, my crew chief said, "I have a star on this medallion my mother gave me. Perhaps you could copy that?" We leapt at this idea – we didn't know one star from another, anyway. But it's an interesting thought that, as a result, the first two 4th FG fighters to fly over occupied France were emblazoned with the Star of David!'

Much of the repainting of the Spitfires at Debden was carried out by US groundcrews newly-arrived in the ETO, these men being reassigned to the group from the 14th FG's 50th FS. The latter unit was due to fly P-38s in the ETO, but had instead been held over indefinitely in Iceland. This left its ground contingent without aircraft at Goxhill, so they were transferred en masse to the 4th FG.

Supermarine Spitfire VB EN853 of the 335th FS/4th FG, Debden, November 1942
Flown by Major 'Jim' Daley, CO of the 335th FS, EN853 was an ex-No 121 Sqn machine employed by the USAAF following the formation of the 4th FG in late September 1942. Both the aircraft and its pilot, 2Lt Chester Grimm, were lost to flak during a bomber escort mission on 22 January 1943.

ABOVE: Ex-No 121 Sqn pilot Don Willis was made Operations Officer of the 335th FS following the former unit's absorption into the USAAF. Having served in the RAF since late 1941, Willis was a vastly experienced pilot who wore no less than four sets of wings on his uniform – Finnish Air Force, Royal Norwegian Air Force, RAF and USAAF. Almost certainly the first US-based volunteer pilot of the Second World War, he had trained with the Finns during the Russo-Finnish war of late 1939, then joined the Royal Norwegian Air Force when Germany invaded in April 1940. Escaping to the UK when Norway fell, Willis eventually made it into the RAF, and then to No 121 Sqn. Tour-expired in 1943, he returned to action the following year, but was shot down in a P-38 and made a PoW until war's end.

RIGHT: Although its serial is hidden by the fighter band, this Spitfire VB is almost certainly EN793, which was the mount of 336th CO Major 'Red' McColpin up until he returned to the US on 28 November 1942. Issued new to No 137 Sqn on 15 June 1942, the fighter was sent to No 121 Sqn just days later, and the Americans in turn passed it on to No 71 Sqn on 28 July. EN793 was transferred to No 306 'Polish' Sqn on 20 August, before finally arriving at No 133 Sqn on 29 September. Damaged on operations on 22 January 1943, the aircraft was re-engined with a Merlin 46 following the 4th FG's re-equipment with P-47s and issued to No 317 'Polish' Sqn on 9 September. The movement merry-go-round continued the following month when EN793 was sent to No 312 'Czech' Sqn. Here it remained until 27 February 1944, when the Spitfire was passed on to No 443 'Canadian' Sqn. Relegated to No 1 TEU on 26 April, EN793 was finally sent to No 61 OTU on 25 June and struck off charge just six days after VE-Day.

LEFT: Armourers work on the port cannon muzzle of a Spitfire VB parked in front of the 336th FS's perimeter HQ shack at Debden in late March 1943. This particular unit was the last to transition to the Thunderbolt within the 4th FG, flying its final operational mission on 10 April. The tiny serial atop the fighter band on this aircraft remains unreadable, thus rendering 'MD-C' unidentifiable.

RIGHT: 2Lt Don Gentile poses in front of his uniquely-marked Spitfire VB BL255 at Debden soon after joining the USAAF in September 1942. A member of the 336th FS, he would go on to become the unit's ranking ace with 21.833 kills by the time he returned to the US in late April 1944. BL255 was the only aircraft that Gentile christened BUCKEYE-DON, its P-47D replacement being called DONNIE BOY and the P-51B that in turn followed in March 1944 bearing the name SHANGRI-LA. All three aircraft were, however, adorned with the boxing eagle motif that eventually became the emblem of the 336th FS. This particular fighter features two kill markings, which denote Gentile's Ju 88 and Fw 190 victories claimed on 19 August 1942 just east of Dieppe. Prior to enjoying a long spell of service firstly with No 133 Sqn and then the 336th FS, BL255 had flown with No 611 Sqn in early 1942. Issued to No 610 Sqn after being discarded by the USAAF in the spring of 1943, the fighter was passed on to No 118 Sqn in the Orkneys in late May 1944 and then back to No 611 Sqn in early October. Just days later BL255 was relegated to training duties with No 61 OTU, and it was struck off charge on 22 May 1945.

Supermarine Spitfire VB BL255 of the 336th FS/4th FG, Debden, October 1942
Decorated with the future emblem of the 336th FS, BL255 was regularly flown by
2Lt Don Gentile during the autumn and winter of 1943-43. The fighter later returned to
RAF control, and saw service with Nos 118, 610 and 611 Sqns.

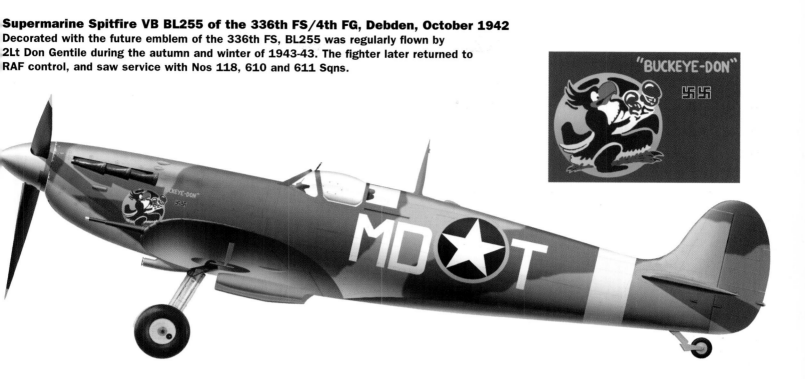

The first wing-strength mission undertaken by the 4th FG took place on 2 October in the
form of Circus 221. The 334th and 335th FSs succeeded in putting up 23 Spitfires, which
joined forces with 31 P-38s of the 1st FG to perform a diversionary sweep from Calais to
Dunkirk whilst Eighth Air Force heavy bombers struck targets further inland. Enemy fighters were
encountered during the mission, and the group claimed four Fw 190s destroyed for no loss.
These were the first victories credited the 'Eagles' since 27 August, and further kills would not
be recorded until late November.

As the weather worsened with the onset of winter, the 4th FG continued in its role as the
sole operational group within VIII Fighter Command. Its pilots flew convoy patrols, Rhubarbs,

LEFT: Pulled off
readiness by visiting
press photographers,
and asked to stand in
front of the 336th FS's
scoreboard, painted on
a wall in the squadron's
operations building,
2Lt Gentile smiles for
the cameras. The many
crosses which adorn
the board denote kills,
probables and damaged
claims credited to the
unit during its time as
No 133 Sqn within RAF
Fighter Command. The
original artwork for the
Air Ministry-approved
squadron crest can also
be seen hanging in a
frame above the eagle.

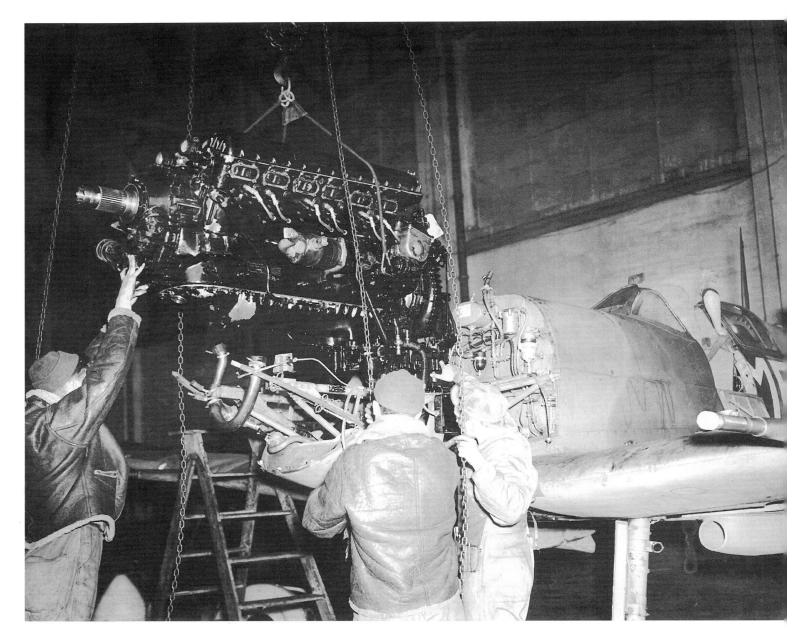

ABOVE: Members of the 4th FG's maintenance section carry out what must have been one of the very last engine changes performed on a Spitfire at Debden. Photographed inside a large C-type hangar at the base in early April 1943, this Mk VB wears the 'MD' codes of the 336th FS. By the end of the month only a solitary example of Supermarine's superlative fighter remained at Debden.

Ramrods and bomber escort missions, although they rarely encountered the enemy. In December Wg Cdr Duke-Woolley was replaced by Lt Col 'Pete' Peterson, and from then on the 4th FG would be both American-manned and led. The previous month, stalwart 'Eagles', and 335th and 336th FS COs, Majs 'Mac' McColpin and 'Jim' Daley had also been reassigned after more than a year on operations. Other volunteer pilots were slowly rotated back to the USA during the first weeks of 1943, whilst heading in the opposite direction were the first examples of the Spitfire's long-awaited replacement – the Republic P-47 Thunderbolt.

The 4th FG's final large-scale fighter engagement with the Spitfire took place on 22 January during Circus 253. Some 25 Spitfires from the 335th and 336th FSs were escorting A-20s heading for the airfield at St Omer when they were intercepted by enemy fighters. In the ensuing engagement four Fw 190s were downed, including one by 336th FS CO, and future ace, Maj Oscar Coen. In return, the group had a single pilot killed when his Spitfire VB was hit by flak.

With the arrival of more and more P-47Cs at Debden, the 4th FG reluctantly started the task of transitioning to the new fighter. On 15 January the 334th was officially taken off operations so that it could act as the Thunderbolt training unit for the group, and the following day the first P-47 was delivered to Debden. By 28 February the unit had almost completed its transition to the Republic fighter, with 11 pilots from all three squadrons within the 4th FG having 30 hours apiece on the P-47. These men were in turn sent back to their respective units the following month to help train their squadronmates.

ABOVE: Although both the 31st and 52nd FGs had departed British shores as long ago as late October 1942, the groups' Spitfire VBs had remained very much in the UK. Some examples were sent to the 4th FG, others reverted back to RAF control, and still more were passed on to the recently-arrived 67th Observation Group (OG), which was assigned to the Eighth Air Force in late September 1942. Although a dedicated tactical reconnaissance unit, the group initially flew unmodified Spitfire VBs so as to allow its pilot to become familiar with their unique low-level mission in the ETO. The 67th OG controlled no fewer than four squadrons at RAF Membury, in Wiltshire, and this former 4th FS/52nd FG aircraft was serving with one of these units when it force-landed near the base on 13 February 1943. Having suffered only modest damage whilst coming to a halt in a freshly-ploughed field, the aircraft was undoubtedly returned to service within weeks of this photograph being taken.

The Spitfire VBs were the most visible link with the 4th FG's 'Eagle' squadron past, and with their replacement just a matter of weeks away, Maj Gen Frank O'D 'Monk' Hunter, Chief of VIII Fighter Command, visited Debden in February 1943. The primary purpose of his visit was to present those volunteer pilots still serving at the base with specially struck RAF medals in the form of miniature lions. During the ceremony he made a brief speech which praised the efforts of the group since its creation:

'Five months ago I came here when the first group of you were transferred to VIII Fighter Command. You will never know what it meant to us to receive a group of fully trained operational pilots.

'You have formed a nucleus around which we have built our fighting machine. We have been able to select men from among you to send to other units to train and lead them. All this, and everything the RAF taught you in three years of fighting the Huns, has been of invaluable aid to us.'

On 16 March the 4th's Spitfire VBs were officially taken off operations, although the 336th FS would continue to fly the Supermarine fighter on convoy patrols until 1 April. Indeed, a handful of Spitfires would maintain readiness at Debden from dawn to dusk for a further ten days. Finally, on the morning of the 10th, the British fighter performed its last mission with the 4th FG when two aircraft completed a convoy patrol. A single Mk VB was retained by the group at Debden as a 'hack' well into the summer of 1943, the weary warrior serving as a reminder to both old and new 'Eagles' of what life had been like as an American volunteer fighter pilot in the RAF in the early years of the war.

'Repulsive Scatterbolt'

The 'Eagle' squadrons and the Spitfire had enjoyed an almost symbiotic association since the autumn of 1941. Although initially equipped with the Hurricane, all three units had seen most of their action, and scored the bulk of their kills, in the Supermarine fighter. They considered it the best aircraft of its type in the world, rivalled only by the German Bf 109 and Fw 190. Their own country had yet to produce a fighter worthy of their patronage, as the near decimation of the USAAF in the Pacific had clearly shown.

However, with the transferring of the 'Eagle' squadrons to USAAF control, the volunteer pilots realised that re-equipment with an American-built fighter was only a matter of months away. And in mid-January 1943 the Spitfire's replacement finally arrived at Debden. Republic's massive Thunderbolt made an immediate impact on the 4th FG, as 'Jim' Goodson recounted in his autobiography, *Over-Paid, Over-Sexed and Over Here*:

'The Thunderbolt, especially after the Spitfire, was huge. It weighed 15,000 lbs to begin with, against the Spit V's 7,100 lbs. For us at least there was no love affair with the P-47 as there had been with the Spitfire. One of the great shocks of the war for me was to get out of my sweet little Spitfire and go over to the great, seven-ton giant which was the P-47 Thunderbolt. After our Spitfires it looked like a Stirling four-engined bomber!

'We might have taken more kindly to it if we hadn't had hours of flying time in the Spit, or even if we had not been hoping to get the P-51 Mustang. I recall a visit from one RAF pilot at Debden. He climbed up on the wing and peered into the P-47's vast cockpit. "Well", he remarked, "I know what the best evasive tactic should be. Just run around the cockpit and hide in one corner!"

BELOW: In March 1943 the Eighth Air Force held a series of press days to help introduce the Thunderbolt to the British public. This particular shot of 334th FS/4th FG P-47C-2 41-6209 was taken by 'Flight's' staff photographer. Standing in front of the big fighter, lending scale to its impressive size, are clutch of 'Fleet Street' reporters and photographers.

LEFT: The old and the new are combined on this 335th FS P-47D-6 (42-74686 'WD-E') adorned with the 'Eagle' squadron emblem. Photographed at Debden on 8 September 1943, this particular aircraft was assigned to the squadron's CO, Maj Roy Evans, whilst the P-47D-1 behind it (42-7863) was flown by Group Ops Officer, Lt Col Don Blakeslee. As denoted by his choice of nose-art, Evans was an ex-No 121 Sqn pilot who had transferred to the USAAF in September 1942. Having claimed a single victory with the Spitfire VB, he went on to score a further four kills with the P-47 during the course o 1943 – his tally with the Thunderbolt can just be made out beneath the windscreen. Evans returned to the USA in February 1944, having completed his tour, although he returned to the ETO in October t fly P-51Ds with the 359th FG. Serving as Deputy Group Commander, Evans claimed a further aerial victory soon after arriving back in the ETO, but wa in turn badly wounded (and captured) when shot down over southern Germany on 14 February 194

LEFT: Maj 'Jim' Goodson (fourth from left in the front row) and his fellow pilots from the 4th FG enjoy a formal dinner with a variety of senior officers in Debden's Officers' Mess on 11 April 1944. Sat opposite Goodson is Supreme Allied Commander, Gen Dwight Eisenhower, whilst to the former's right is Lt Gen James Doolittle, Commander of the Eighth Air Force. Sat alongside Gen Eisenhower, pouring a cup of coffee, is Lt Col Don Blakeslee, who is in conversation with Gen Carl Spaatz, Commander US Strategic Air Forces in Europe. To Spaatz's left is Capt Don Gentile, who, along with Blakeslee, had been awarded a DSC earlier in the day in recognition of him becoming the Eighth Air Force's then leading ace. Finally, the senior officer sat second from left immediately in front of the large window is Maj Gen William Kepner, Commander of VIII Fighter Command.

ABOVE: One of the best Allied fighter leaders of the Second World War, Don Blakeslee prepares for yet another sortie in his beloved Spitfire VB whilst serving with No 133 Sqn. Awarded a DFC during his tour with No 401 Sqn in 1941-42, he was posted to the 'Eagle' squadron in June 1942 as a replacement for 'Red' McColpin, who had returned to the USA on a ten-week War Bond tour. Having sortied four times in support of the Dieppe raid, he was made acting CO of No 133 Sqn when its former boss was promoted to wing leader. However, within days of taking command, Blakeslee was 'busted' back to the rank of a pilot officer and posted out of No 11 Group when he was caught with two WAAFs in his quarters after hours by the station commander at Martlesham Heath! His banishment only ended with the formation of the 4th FG, for the group's executive operations officer, Lt Col 'Pete' Peterson, had requested that he be brought in to lead one of the new USAAF units. The final decision on Blakeslee's future was left to Maj Gen 'Monk' Hunter, head of VIII Fighter Command. An ex-cavalry officer, and confirmed bachelor, Hunter's reply to Peterson was, 'Did you say two women? And you suggest that he becomes a major? Hell, I'll make him a colonel'. Blakeslee never looked back.

'However, with time and experience, we came to have a grudging respect for the big "Thunderjug". Certainly considering its size and weight, this fighter had an amazing performance, particularly at altitude. It was faster than the Spitfire V and, of course, in a dive nothing could touch it.

'I remember discussing the plane with Don Blakeslee. "Well, Don, at least the 109s and 190s won't be able to dive away from us anymore. This plane will catch anything in a dive". "Well", he replied, "It damn well ought to be able to dive – it sure as Hell can't climb!"'

The first 'Eagle' squadron ace, Bill Dunn, also saw action with the P-47 as part of the USAAF's Ninth Air Force in 1944;

'The Repulsive Scatterbolt, we called it. It had a lot of nicknames, most of them nasty. They were big mothers. The first time I saw one of them, I asked, "Where in hell is the other engine?"

The 4th FG's commanding officer when the first P-47s arrived at Debden was Lt Col 'Pete' Peterson, who had been on active service with the 'Eagle' squadrons since November 1940. Probably the most experienced US fighter pilot in England by early 1943, he had amassed over 400 hours of operational flying in Hurricanes and Spitfires by the time he came to convert onto the Thunderbolt;

'I was not really impressed with the P-47. It did turn out to be an exceptionally fine airplane, but not necessarily as a high-altitude escort fighter, which was my business. Men who had been flying smaller planes like the Spitfire, or even the P-40, found the P-47 to be a great big chunk of metal that wasn't exactly what they thought of as a fighter. Therefore, it wasn't really impressive from the standpoint of the pure joy of flying.

'Of course, being a comparatively new airplane, it had an awful lot of maintenance bugs and problems. The engine would quit at odd times. The supercharger wouldn't work here and there. Normal bugs, but they destroyed the pilot's confidence in the airplane, which he desperately needed to have in order to fight with it effectively.'

RIGHT: CO of No 71 Sqn at just 21 years of age, and then group commander of the 4th FG by 23, Chesley Gordon 'Pete' Peterson was one of the most experienced American 'Eagles' in the ETO by the time the first P-47s arrived at Debden. He was also the only American fighter pilot to be awarded a British DSO. Brow furrowed and hands on hips, Peterson watches intently as his fitter works on the Merlin engine in his Hurricane II in 1941.

RAF 'Eagles'

Not all American volunteer pilots chose to fight with the 'Eagle' squadrons upon their formation in 1940-41. Indeed, well over 50 individuals remained in various units within the frontline commands, the survivors returning to the USA once their tours were up. In this chapter, the Spitfires of a select few notable pilots are featured both photographically and in profile. These represent just a fraction of the aircraft flown by those Americans who saw action with Fighter Command outside of the 'Eagle' squadron set up between 1941 and 1943.

BELOW: 'A Yank in the RAF' was shot at Prestwick, on the west coast of Scotland, with filming taking a full month to complete. No 602 Sqn had been one of Fighter Command's most successful units during the Battle of Britain, but had not had a single 'Yank' serve within its ranks throughout 1940! However, the unit had been pulled out of the frontline in December 1940 and sent to Prestwick for rest and recuperation, thus making it the ideal candidate for film work. In this shot, squadron pilots scramble en masse from their 'Old Mill' HQ building to awaiting Spitfire IAs parked in the nearby dispersal. All this activity is being eagerly filmed by a cameraman in the foreground, with attendant 'extras' watching on.

LEFT: The aerial war in Europe was given the Hollywood treatment in March 1941 when a crew from 20th Century Productions filmed the activities of No 602 'City of Glasgow' Sqn for inclusion in the motion picture, 'A Yank in the RAF'. This was America's first attempt at covering the conflict taking place across the Atlantic, and it would spawn a series of copycat films that focused on US volunteer pilots in the RAF, including Ronald Reagan's 'International Squadron' (1941) by Warner Brothers, and Universal Pictures' 'Eagle Squadron' (1941). All three proved to be little more than propaganda vehicles, and the latter film was dismissed out of hand by the members of the real 'Eagle' squadrons after they had sat through its British premiere in London. 'That movie upset everybody, and Sqn Ldr Peterson in particular', No 71 Sqn pilot Bill Geiger stated after the war. 'We had been told that it would be a documentary. It came to all of us as a great shock when it turned out to be very third-rate. We all felt that we had been double-crossed'.

Supermarine Spitfire IA (serial unknown) of No 602 'City of Glasgow' Sqn, Prestwick, March 1941
This aircraft participated in the filming of *A Yank in the RAF*, which was shot by 20th Century Productions at Prestwick during March 1941.

BELOW: Another still in the sequence taken on the day of the great scramble 'shoot' at Prestwick in March 1941. This views shows two No 602 Sqn pilots preparing to strap into their already idling Spitfire IAs. The pilot closest to the camera is already clambering over the cockpit sill into his 'office', whilst his section mate is still wrestling with the buttons on his 'Mae West'. The flying sequences shot for 'A Yank in the RAF' were amongst the best taken during the entire war, and edited segments appeared in other feature films of this period, including 'Mrs Miniver', 'Battle of Britain' and 'Dangerous Moonlight'.

RIGHT: Looking every inch the fighter pilot, a young Plt Off Don Blakeslee pauses for the camera prior to easing himself into the cockpit of his Spitfire VB (BL753) at Gravesend in May 1942. A graduate of the British Commonwealth Air Training Plan, Blakeslee had been in the frontline with No 401 'Ram' Sqn RCAF since the autumn of 1941. He had claimed one Bf 109 destroyed, three damaged and two Fw 190s probably destroyed by the spring of 1942, although he refrained from adorning his fighter with any form of personal scoreboard - he did, however, name BL753 LEOLA in honour of his wife. Blakeslee refused to allow his various crew chiefs to apply nicknames, kill markings, 'girlie' art or personal insignia to his aircraft upon joining the 4th FG, despite having increased his score to 14 destroyed by July 1944.

Supermarine Spitfire VB BL753 of No 401 'Ram' Sqn RCAF, Gravesend, May 1942
Flown regularly by Plt Off Don Blakeslee during his spell with the Canadian fighter squadron, this aircraft bore the name *LEOLA* below its cockpit in honour of the pilot's wife. Delivered new to No 401 Sqn RCAF, BL753 later served with Nos 65, 132 and 316 Sqns, before being shot down by flak while spotting for naval gunfire over Bayeux on 25 June 1944. It was assigned to No 63 Sqn at the time.

ABOVE: Wearing his trademark white scarf, Plt Off Don Blakeslee of No 411 'Grizzly Bear' Sqn RCAF (seventh from the right) poses with his fellow pilots at RAF Digby in late May 1942. Serving with this unit for just a matter of weeks, Blakeslee would soon be posted to No 121 Sqn. Fellow Americans Plt Off W F Ash (smoking a cigarette, second from left in the front row) and Sgt John McFarlane (standing, second from left) can also be seen in this group shot. The latter pilot eventually followed Blakeslee to the 4th FG, serving with the 336th FS from 28 June 1944 through to 12 March 1945. McFarlane ended the war with the rank of major, having been the 336th's Operations Officer for much of his time with the unit. His tour was cut short when he was forced to bail out of his Mustang due to engine failure whilst leading a group of fighters on a bomber escort mission to Swinemünde, in northern Germany, on 12 March 1945. McFarlane, who claimed one aerial victory and three strafing kills during his time with the 4th FG, successfully avoided capture by evading through Sweden.

BELOW: The first American to turn his back on the 'Eagles' was Plt Off 'Art' Donahue, who had initially been an early recruit for No 71 Sqn in late September 1940. He was posted to the newly-formed unit from No 64 Sqn, where he had seen several weeks of fighting during the Battle of Britain. Fed up with no flying due to No 71 Sqn's lack of aircraft, Donahue requested a transfer back to his old unit in late October. He confessed to a fellow American volunteer pilot some months later that he considered the 'Eagles' 'a motley crew that would never amount to anything'. Donahue flew a considerable number of sorties with No 64 Sqn from Hornchurch up until he transferred to No 91 'Nigeria' Sqn in late February 1941. The latter unit was based at Hawkinge, from where it had established an enviable reputation as a specialist armed reconnaissance squadron. This particular Spitfire II was delivered new to No 91 Sqn in April 1941, and although it remained with the unit for just a month, it is likely that Donahue flew P8194 at least once during this time.

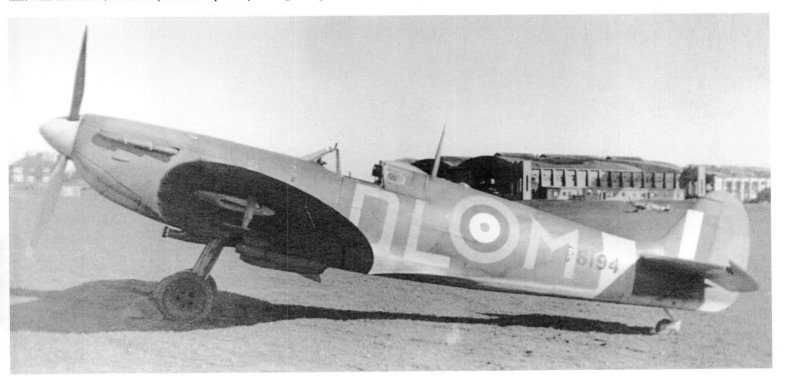

ABOVE: Posing with No 91 Sqn's 'B' Flight at Hawkinge on 21 October 1941, Flg Off 'Art' Donahue can be seen standing with his hands in his pockets third from right. Fellow American Sgt Appleton (forename unknown) stands at the far left. No 91 Sqn seemed to be a popular posting for 'foreign' pilots, with the shoulder flashes of Canada, the USA, Australia, New Zealand, South Africa, France, Belgium, Norway, the Netherlands, Rhodesia and South Africa regularly being spotted in the various messes at Hawkinge.

BELOW: No 91 Sqn's 'B' Flight is seen lined up for an inspection at Hawkinge in May 1942. The pilot standing nearest to the camera is Sqn Ldr 'Bobby' Oxspring, who had been in command of the unit since January of that year. When 'Art' Donahue returned to the 'Nigeria' squadron in August 1942, he assumed command of this flight after its previous commander, Flt Lt 'Billy' Orr, had been lost on operations on 22 July.

ABOVE: By the time this photograph was taken in late August 1942, 'Art' Donahue (extreme left) had been promoted to flight lieutenant and awarded the DFC. He had also seen action flying Hurricanes with No 258 Sqn in the Far East during the ill-fated defence of Singapore and Sumatra. Former 'Eagle' John Campbell served with Donahue in No 258 Sqn, and remembers that he 'was an idealist – one of the few real ones in the squadron. He had high principles. His former flight commander once told me Art had tried to resign his commission so he could be a sergeant pilot. Donahue felt he should be no more privileged than any other fighter pilot in the squadron'. The author of two wartime autobiographies, the first American-based volunteer pilot to see service with Fighter Command, and a veteran of two frontline tours, 'Art' Donahue was posted missing in action on 11 September 1942. He had sortied alone at dawn and headed for the Belgian coast in an effort to ensnare a German nightfighter by flying slowly like a bomber. Donahue's trap worked, and whilst engaging a Ju 88 his Spitfire VB was hit by return fire and he was forced to bail out in bad weather. His body was never found.

Supermarine Spitfire VB (serial unknown) of No 91 'Nigeria' Sqn, Hawkinge, August 1942
Bearing distinctive artwork beneath the cockpit, this aircraft was the mount of American pilot Sgt A C Younge, who flew with No 91 Sqn's 'B' Flight for much of 1942.

RIGHT: Sgt A C 'Bud' Younge of Cleveland, Ohio, served briefly with 'Art' Donahue in 'B' Flight during the latter pilot's second spell with No 91 Sqn. Also seen sat on the wing of his Spitfire VB in the photograph published on the previous page, the American pilot seemingly called all his aircraft MY MARIAN – this nickname is visible both on CLEVELAND'S CHALLENGE! and the fighter in the background of the group shot.

BELOW: This classic Charles E Brown photograph from May 1942 shows No 222 Sqn Spitfire VB AD233 in flight over Essex during a training sortie from North Weald. The fighter has been adorned with a small rank pennant just below the windscreen, denoting its assignment to the unit's CO, Battle of Britain ace Sqn Ldr 'Dickie' Milne. When the latter pilot finished his tour in May 1942, AD233 was passed to Sqn Ldr Jerzy Jankiewicz, who duly became the first Pole to command a British-manned fighter unit. Also a Battle of Britain veteran Jankiewicz had served with No 601 Sqn in 1940, where he had fought alongside American Carl Davis up until the latter pilot's death on 6 September 1940. The Pole's period in command of No 222 Sqn was to last just 72 hours, however, for on 25 May 1942 he was shot down and killed in AD233 by Fw 190s from JG 26 during Rodeo 51. His replacement at No 222 Sqn was ex-Chicago newspaper reporter, Sqn Ldr 'Newt' Anderson, who had been posted in from No 71 Sqn. The first American to lead a British-manned fighter unit, Anderson was in turn killed in action (again by JG 26) on 29 June 1942 whilst leading the North Weald Wing during Circus 195.

ABOVE: When No 611 'West Lancashire' Sqn traded in its weary Spitfire VBs for brand new Spitfire IXCs in late July 1942, it became one of the first units in Fighter Command to receive the vastly improved version of Supermarine's frontline fighter. Based at Redhill at the time, the squadron moved further east to Biggin Hill on 23 September, where it was soon able to demonstrate the aircraft's clear superiority over all other RAF fighters then in service. Essentially a Mk V airframe fitted with a two-speed, two-stage supercharged Merlin 61, the re-engined Mk IX had a top speed of 408 mph, compared with its predecessor's 357 mph. Flying the latest variant of Spitfire, and based at No 11 Group's most famous fighter station, No 611 Sqn was regularly visited by the press during the late summer of 1942, and this shot was taken on just such an occasion soon after the Mk IXs had arrived in Kent.

Supermarine Spitfire F IXC EN133 of No 611 'West Lancashire' Sqn, Biggin Hill, September 1942
Occasionally flown by Austrian American Flt Lt Franz Colloredo-Mansfeld, EN133 was one of the first F IXCs built. It remained with the unit until shot down off the coast of France by Fw 190s from II./JG 26 on 14 March 1943.

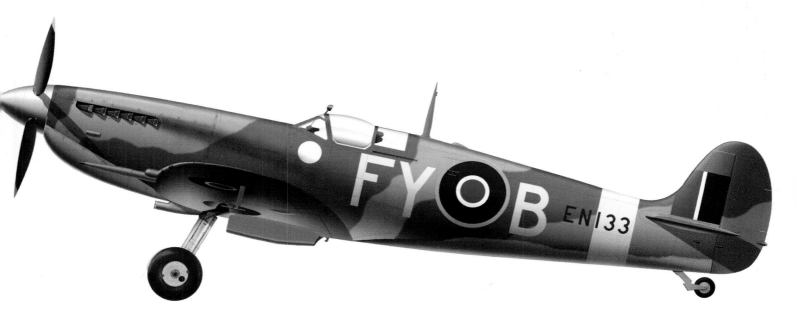

ABOVE: Parked in the middle distance of the photograph run on the previous page is Spitfire F IXC EN133, which was inspected by the press soon after its arrival at Biggin Hill in late November 1942. At that stage the white disc painted just below the windscreen still lacked any artwork, and the fighter's overall finish was very much ex-factory. However, by the time this photograph was taken in February 1943, the Spitfire had seen almost three months of continual action, and its external appearance reflected this. Note also that the disc now boasts artwork, although of exactly what remains a mystery – could it be a head and shoulders view of Britain's illustrious Prime Minister, Winston Churchill, depicted in a typical cigar-smoking pose? The fighter also carried the name 'Miriam' in faded letters just forward of the artwork.

ABOVE: The American connection within No 611 Sqn at this time was senior flight commander Flt Lt Franz Colloredo-Mansfeld, who is seen here in the centre of the photograph with his left hand on the propeller blade. This shot was taken to mark the occasion of the 1000th kill scored by fighters flying from Biggin Hill, on 15 May 1943, the first victory having been scored by American 'Jimmy' Davies of No 79 Sqn back in November 1939. An Austrian who had fled to the USA with his parents in the early 1930s following the rise of Nazism in neighbouring Germany, Colloredo-Mansfeld had returned to Europe in 1941 in order to fly with the RAF. Nicknamed 'Collie' in the air force, Colloredo-Mansfeld was a wealthy individual who enjoyed giving his friends presents – including an MG sportscar to Kiwi ace, and squadronmate, Johnny Checketts! He had served with No 72 Sqn during the summer of 1942, prior to being posted as a flight commander to No 611 Sqn at year-end. Colloredo-Mansfeld enjoyed great success with the Spitfire IX, claiming three kills, three probables and four damaged between January and July 1943. Awarded a DFC for his fighting qualities, 'Collie' was made CO of No 132 Sqn in August of that year, and he remained in command until he was shot down and killed by flak whilst flying out over the French coast on 7 January 1944.

LEFT: On 9 December 1942, No 611 Sqn sortied all 12 of its Spitfire F IXCs for the visiting press at Biggin Hill. This particular shot was taken by a 'Flight' photographer standing alongside the main runway at the base, and it shows the final four-ship in the formation heading north-west in the direction of the Salt Box, and Bromley.

BELOW: A handful of photographers also got airborne on 9 December, including Charles E Brown, who took this fantastic shot as the squadron flew over the urban sprawl of South London. After taking a series of photos showing the aircraft in a loose diamond formation astern, Brown and his contemporaries then worked with the lead four-ship of fighters, headed by the unit's Australian CO, Sqn Ldr Hugo 'Sinker' Armstrong, in 'FY-F' (BS435). EN199 was also included in this quartet, the aircraft boasting an unpainted replacement wing root panel which undoubtedly caused some gnashing of teeth within the squadron's engineering section when they saw the results of the sortie! Armstrong and BS435 were lost on 5 February 1943 when his small flight of three fighters tangled with eight Fw 190s of 5./JG 26 at low-level off Boulogne. EN199, and its pilot, Sqn Ldr J H Slater, fell victim to II./JG 26 over the French coast just weeks later on 14 March whilst participating in Rodeo 188.

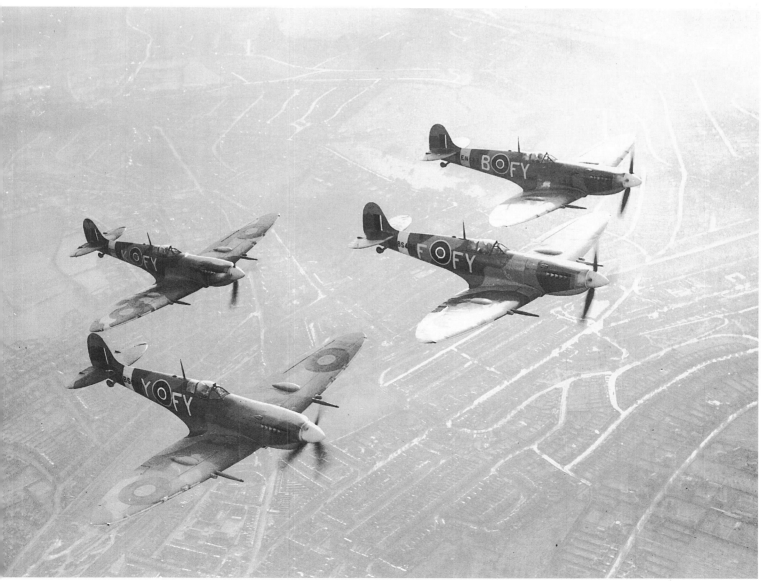

RIGHT: One of the few serving USAAF fighter pilots to see action with the RAF after the establishment of the Eighth Air Force was Francis Gabreski, who would later become the leading American ace in the ETO. Of Polish ancestry, and a fluent speaker of the language, he somehow convinced his superiors that he should be posted to a Polish unit in the RAF in order to gain combat experience prior to the arrival of other USAAF units in the UK. Gabreski arrived in England (from Hawaii, via Washington, D.C.) in October 1942, and then spent the next two months ferrying all manner of USAAF aircraft to various bases in the UK. After a chance encounter with Polish pilots in a London club, Gabreski was finally sent to No 315 'City of Deblin' Sqn at RAF Northolt in December 1942. He subsequently flew eleven combat and two air-search and rescue missions with the unit, before being posted to the Eighth Air Force's 56th FG. As a captain, 'Gabby' Gabreski is seen climbing out of the cockpit of Spitfire F IXC BS410 'PK-E' at the end of his first mission (Circus 252), flown on 21 January 1943.

LEFT: Two Polish pilots from No 315 Sqn pose on the tailplane of Spitfire F IXC BS513, which was flown by 'Gabby' Gabreski on several occasions whilst 'learning the ropes' at Northolt. The future Eighth Air Force 'ace of aces' made the following comment after his first flight in this aircraft: 'By the time I landed at Northolt I understood why the RAF had decided not to use any of the P-40s we had sent them on lend-lease for combat over Europe. The Spitfire was in a whole different league, and so apparently were the Luftwaffe's fighters.'

Supermarine Spitfire F IXC EN172 of No 315 'City of Deblin' Sqn, Northolt, January 1943
Flown by future ranking USAAF ETO ace Francis 'Gabby' Gabreski during his brief spell with Polish-manned No 315 Sqn in early 1943, this aircraft was assigned to unit CO, Sqn Ldr Tadeusz Sawicz. It wears the unit's cockerel badge below the windscreen.

ABOVE: Within weeks of Gabreski leaving Northolt for the P-47-equipped 56th FG, No 315 Sqn was replaced at the Middlesex fighter station by No 316 'City of Warsaw' Sqn. Leaving No 11 Group for a period of rest and recuperation also meant parting with its beloved Spitfire F IXCs, which remained at Northolt for the incoming unit. This particular No 316 Sqn aircraft (BS456) was actually an ex-No 306 'City of Torun' Sqn machine, the latter unit serving in the Northolt Wing concurrently with No 315 Sqn during 'Gabby' Gabreski's spell in the RAF. BS456 was downed by Fw 190s during a No 316 Sqn Ramrod flown on the evening 22 August 1943, its pilot (Flt Lt L Kurylowicz) spending five days in his dinghy prior to being rescued.

ABOVE: Capt Francis Gabreski poses in his USAAF uniform alongside a No 308 'City of Krakow' Sqn Spitfire VB in January 1943. This unit was a part of the Northolt Wing at the same time as No 315 Sqn, whom Gabreski flew with.

ABOVE RIGHT: Two of the three Spitfire F IXCs seen in this photograph were flown operationally by Capt Gabreski. EN172/ 'PK-K' was his mount on the 4 February 1943 Rodeo to St Omer, whilst BS513/'PK-Z' was also used by him on sweeps over France.

RIGHT: Another unit at Northolt during Gabreski's time with the Poles was No 306 'City of Torun' Sqn.

LEFT: Rather than ending this book with an American in a Spitfire, here we have a Spitfire in America! This F IXC (MK210) was one of two Supermarine fighters modified by engineers at Wright Field, in Ohio, the aircraft having all available interior space converted into fuel tanks, and two P-51 drop tanks plumbed in under the wings. Both Spitfires successfully crossed the Atlantic in this configuration in mid-1944.

Bibliography

Allen, H R 'Dizzy'. *Battle for Britain.* Corgi, London, 1975

Baker, David. *Adolf Galland.* Windrow & Greene, London, 1996

Baxter, G G, K A Owen and P Baldock. *Aircraft Casualties in Kent, Part 1.* Meresborough Books, Rainham, 1990

Bowyer, Michael J F. *Fighting Colours.* PSL, London, 1969

Bowyer, Michael J F. *Aircraft for the Few.* PSL, Sparkford, 1991

Bowyer, Chaz. *Fighter Command.* J M Dent & Sons, London, 1980

Bowyer, Chaz. *Bristol Blenheim.* Ian Allan, London, 1984

Bowyer, Chaz. *Fighter Pilots of the RAF 1939-45.* William Kimber, London, 1984

Bracken, Robert. *Spitfire - The Canadians.* The Boston Mills Press, Erin, 1995

Brooks, Robin J. *Sussex Airfields in the Second World War.* Countryside Books, Newbury, 1993

Brooks, Robin J. *Kent Airfields in the Second World War.* Countryside Books, Newbury, 1998

Caine, Philip D. *American Pilots in the RAF.* Brassey's (US), Washington, D.C., 1993

Caldwell, Donald. *The JG 26 War Diary, Volume One.* Grub Street, London, 1996

Caldwell, Donald. *The JG 26 War Diary, Volume Two.* Grub Street, London, 1998

Cameron, Dugald. *Glasgow's Own.* Squadron Prints, Glasgow, 1987

Childers, James Saxon. *War Eagles.* William Heinemann, London, 1943

Collier, Richard. *Eagle Day.* Pan Books, London, 1968

Cormack, Andrew. *Men-at-Arms 225 - The Royal Air Force 1939-45.* Osprey, London, 1990

Crook, D M. *Spitfire Pilot.* Faber and Faber, London, 1942

Cull, Brian et al. *Twelve Days in May.* Grub Street, London, 1995

Donahue, Arthur Gerald. *Tally-Ho!* MacMillan and Co, London, 1941

Flint, Peter. *R.A.F. Kenley.* Terence Dalton, Lavenham, 1985

Franks, Norman. *Wings of Freedom.* William Kimber, London, 1980

Franks, Norman. *The Greatest Air Battle.* Grub Street, London, 1992

Franks, Norman and Paul Richey. *Fighter Pilot's Summer.* Grub Street, London, 1993

Franks, Norman. *Fighter Command Losses, Volume 1.* Midland Publishing, Leicester, 1997

Franks, Norman. *Fighter Command Losses, Volume 2.* Midland Publishing, Leicester, 1998

Franks, Norman. *Air Battle Dunkirk.* Grub Street, London, 2000

Franks, Norman and Mike O'Connor. *Number One in War and Peace.* Grub Street, London, 2000

Freeman, Roger A. *The Mighty Eighth.* McDonald and Jane's, London, 1978

Freeman, Roger A. *Mighty Eighth War Diary.* Jane's, London, 1981

Freeman, Roger A. *Airfields of the Eighth Then and Now.* After the Battle Publications, London, 1986

Fry, Garry L and Jeffrey L Ethell. *Escort to Berlin.* ARCO, New York, 1980

Gabreski, Francis (as told to Carl Molesworth). *Gabby - A Fighter Pilot's Life.* Orion Books, New York, 1991

Gardner, Charles. *AASF.* Hutchinson & Co, London, 1940

Gelb, Norman. *Scramble.* Michael Joseph, London, 1986

Goodrum, Alastair. *Combat Ready!* GNS Enterprises, Peterborough, 1997

Goodson, James A. *Tumult in the Clouds.* Arrow Books, London, 1986

Goodson, James A and Norman Franks. *Over-Paid, Over-Sexed and Over Here.* Wingham Press, Canterbury, 1991

Goss, Chris. *Brothers in Arms.* Crécy Books, Manchester, 1994

Goulding, James and Richard L Ward. *Camouflage & Markings - Gladiator, Gauntlet, Fury, Demon.* Ducimus Books, London, 1971

Goulding, James. *Camouflage & Markings - Hawker Hurricane.* Ducimus Books, London, 1971

Goulding, James. *Camouflage & Markings - Supermarine Spitfire.* Ducimus Books, London, 1971

Goulding, James. *Camouflage & Markings - Bristol Blenheim.* Ducimus Books, London, 1971

Gretzyngier, Robert and Wojtek Matusiak. *Aircraft of the Aces 21 - Polish Aces of World War 2.* Osprey Aerospace Publishing, London, 1998

Haugland, Vern. *The Eagle Squadrons.* David & Charles, Newton Abbot, 1979

Haugland, Vern. *The Eagles' War.* Jason Aronson, New York, 1982

Halley, James J. *RAF Aircraft L1000 - N9999.* Air-Britain, Tonbridge, 1993

Halley, James J. *RAF Aircraft P1000 - R9999.* Air-Britain, Tunbridge Wells, 1996

Halley, James J. *RAF Aircraft W1000 - Z9999.* Air-Britain, Tunbridge Wells, 1998

Halley, James J. *RAF Aircraft AA100 - AZ999.* Air-Britain, Tunbridge Wells, 2000

Halley, James J. *RAF Aircraft BA100 - BZ999.* Air-Britain, Tonbridge, 1986

Halley, James J. *RAF Aircraft EA100 - EZ999.* Air-Britain, Tonbridge, 1988

Halley, James J. *The K File.* Air-Britain, Tunbridge Wells, 1995

Hess, William N and Thomas G Ivie. *Fighter sof the Mighty Eighth.* Motorbooks, Osceola, 1990

Holmes, Tony. *Aircraft of the Aces 18 - Hurricane Aces 1939-40.* Osprey Aerospace Publishing, London, 1998

Humphreys, Roy. *RAF Hawkinge in Old Photographs.* Alan Sutton, Stroud, 1991

Hunt, Leslie. *Twenty-One Squadrons.* Garnstone Press, London, 1972

Jefford, C G. *RAF Squadrons.* Airlife Publishing, Shrewsbury, 1994

Kennerly, Byron. *The Eagles Roar!* Zenger, Washington, D.C., 1980

Klinkowitz, Jerome. *Yanks over Europe.* The University Press of Kentucky, 1996
Kucera, Dennis C. *In a Now Forgotten Sky.* Flying Machine Press, Stratford, 1997

Leal, H J T. *Battle in the Skies over the Isle of Wight.* Isle of Wight County Press, Newport, 1996

Lucas, Laddie (edited by). *Wings of War.* Hutchinson, London, 1984

Lucas, Paul. *Camouflage and Markings 2 - The Battle For Britain - RAF.* Scale Aircraft Monographs, Luton, 2000

Ludwig, Paul and Malcolm Laird. *American Spitfire, Part One.* Ventura Publications, Wellington, 1998

Ludwig, Paul and Malcolm Laird. *American Spitfire, Part Two.* Ventura Publications, Wellington, 1999

Lumsden, Alec and Owen Thetford. *On Silver Wings.* Osprey Aerospace Publishing, London, 1993

Mason, Frank. *Profile Publications Number 10 – The Gloster Gauntlet.* Profile Publications, Leatherhead, 1965

Mason, Frank. *The Hawker Hurricane.* Aston Publications, Bourne End, 1987

Mason, Frank. *Battle over Britain.* Aston Publications, Bourne End, 1990

McIntosh, Dave. *High Blue Battle.* Spa Books, Stevenage, 1990

McRoberts, Douglas. *Lions Rampant.* William Kimber, London, 1986

Michulec, Robert. *Werner "Vati" Mölders.* Mushroom Model Publications, Redbourn, 2000

Minterne, Don. *The History of 73 Squadron, Part 1.* Tutor Publications, Dorchester, 1994

Monks, Noel. *Squadrons Up!* Whittlesey House, New York, 1941

Morgan, Eric B and Edward Shacklady, *Spitfire – The History.* Key Publishing, Stamford, 1993

Moulson, Tom. *The Flying Sword.* Macdonald, London, 1964

Ogley, Bob. *Biggin on the Bump.* Froglets Publications, Westerham, 1990

Olynyk, Frank. *Stars & Bars.* Grub Street, London, 1995
Orange, Vincent. *The Road to Biggin Hill.* Airlife Publishing, Shrewsbury, 1986

Oxspring, Bobby. *Spitfire Command.* William Kimber, London, 1984

Pilkington, Len. *Surrey Airfields in the Second World War.* Countryside Books, Newbury, 1997

Price, Dr Alfred. *Battle of Britain Day.* Sidgwick & Jackson, London, 1990

Price, Dr Alfred. *Aircraft of the Aces 5 – Late Mark Spitfire Aces.* Osprey Aerospace Publishing, London, 1995

Price, Dr Alfred. *Aircraft of the Aces 12 – Spitfire Mark I/II Aces 1939-41.* Osprey Aerospace Publishing, London, 1996

Prodger, Mick J. *Luftwaffe vs RAF, Part 1.* Schiffer Military History, Atglen, 1997

Prodger, Mick J. *Luftwaffe vs RAF, Part 2.* Schiffer Military History, Atglen, 1998

Ramsey, Winston G (edited by). *The Battle of Britain Then and Now, Mk IV.* After the Battle Publications, London, 1987

Rawlings, J. *Fighter Squadrons of the RAF and their Aircraft.* Crécy, Manchester, 1993

Richey, Paul. *Fighter Pilot.* Jane's, London, 1980

Robertson, Bruce. *Spitfire – The Story of a Famous Fighter,* Harleyford Publications, Letchworth, 1960

Saunders, Andy. *RAF Tangmere in Old Photographs.* Universal Books, Hoo, 1998

Saunders, Andy. *RAF Tangmere Revisted.* Alan Sutton, Stroud, 1998

Shaw, Michael. *No 1 Squadron.* Ian Allan, London, 1986

Shores, Christopher et al. *Fledgling Eagles.* Grub Street, London, 1991

Shores, Christopher and Clive Williams. *Aces High.* Grub Street, London, 1994

Shores, Christopher and Clive Williams. *Aces High Vol. 2,* Grub Street, London, 1999

Stones, Donald. *Dimsie.* Wingham Press, Canterbury, 1991

Sturtivant, Ray et al. *Royal Air Force Flying Training and Support Units.* Air-Britain, Tunbridge Wells, 1997
Thetford, Owen. *Aircraft of the Royal Air Force 1918-57.* Putnam, London, 1957

Vasco, John J. *Bombsights Over England.* JAC Publications, Norwich, 1990

Vasco, John J and Peter D Cornwell. *Zerstörer.* JAC Publications, Norwich, 1995

Wynn, Kenneth G. *Men of the Battle of Britain.* CCB Associates, South Croydon, 1999

Wallace, Graham. *RAF Biggin Hill.* Putnam, London, 1957

Ziegler, Frank H. *The Story of 609 Squadron.* Crécy, Manchester, 1993

Zielinski, Jozef. *Polish Airmen in the Battle of Britain.* Oficyna Wydawnicza, Warsaw, 1999